Kingdom Expressions

Kingdom Expressions

Trends Influencing the
Advancement of the Gospel

J. D. Payne

THOMAS NELSON
Since 1798

NASHVILLE   DALLAS   MEXICO CITY   RIO DE JANEIRO

Other Books by J. D. Payne

Missional House Churches: Reaching Our Communities with the Gospel

Discovering Church Planting: An Introduction to the Whats, Whys, and Hows of Global Church Planting

The Barnabas Factors: Eight Essential Practices of Church Planting Team Members

Evangelism: A Biblical Response to Today's Questions

Published in Nashville, Tennessee, by Thomas Nelson. Thomas Nelson is a registered trademark of Thomas Nelson, Inc.

Thomas Nelson, Inc., titles may be purchased in bulk for educational, business, fundraising, or sales promotional use. For information, please e-mail SpecialMarkets@ ThomasNelson.com.

Typesetting by Kevin A. Wilson, Upper Case Textual Services, Lawrence, MA

ISBN 978-1-4185-4596-3

Printed in the United States of America

12 13 14 15 16 QG 6 5 4 3 2 1

To the Lord, who allows kingdom expressions for his glory
and
to Sarah, an amazing expression of his love to me

Contents

Preface

During the twentieth century and first decade of the twenty-first century, American Evangelicals observed the rise of unique trends and movements. Many of these new religious expressions developed from deep convictions regarding the missionary nature of the church. Evangelicals wrestled deeply with how to better evangelize the nations, both across the street and across the world. What started with a heightened evangelistic zeal among a few people oftentimes developed into movements to advance the gospel, with large numbers of participants and abundant resources. While many individuals and churches participating in these new expressions remained loyal to their denominations, these new trends and movements were not bound to a single denomination. They often developed and matured outside of any one denominational authority.

The purpose of this book is to focus on several of the most influential expressions of missionary-type movements among evangelicals, which developed out of a distinctly missionary zeal to carry out the Great Commission by making disciples of all nations (Matt. 28:18–20). The parameters of this book are to focus on those expressions that have shaped and influenced the church in the United States in particular. Seventeen years as an evangelical minister, educator, and missiologist provide me wisdom as an authoritative source on such matters that should be included in this work.

However, books in general are always limited by length. And a reference book, in particular, is rarely exhaustive and highly influenced by the author's background and interests at the moment. I know that some readers will immediately identify omissions in this book upon examining the table of contents. For example, this book does not address the Signs and Wonders Movement, a movement that had great influence and garnered much attention in the evangelical world. But even with the noticeable lack of expressions deserving recognition, I think you will find this book to be of assistance to you.

Each of the expressions discussed in this book share common threads. As you read, please keep in mind the following commonalities. First, all of these movements and trends have evangelical roots and are currently taking place (or have taken place) within evangelical churches. And like the greater American Evangelicalism, there is a wide theological spectrum represented. Also, the emphasis on evangelical roots should not cause you to assume that mainline, Catholic, or Orthodox churches avoided or failed to contribute to such expressions. For example, there were many mainline contributions to the Missional Church Movement, and many mainline, Catholic, and Orthodox contributions to the Emergent group connected to the Emerging Church Movement.

Second, the expressions addressed in this book are not exclusive to a particular denomination. It would be best to state that they are transdenominational (involving many denominations) and nondenominational (of no one denomination). It should be observed that the influence of these expressions has been carried over into various denominations. An example of this would be the networks of developing cowboy churches that are Southern Baptist in their affiliation.

Third, the expressions examined in this book are not necessarily mutually exclusive. At times there is much overlap among them. For example, the Spiritual Warfare Movement was highly influenced by elements of the Church Growth Movement. The Missional Church Movement has extended its influence in a multitude of areas, including into the Multisite Church Movement, among numerous church planting networks, Emerging Church Movement, and the Cowboy Church Movement, just to name a few. Many megachurches are also multisite churches. The Lausanne Movement has had an impact on most of those movements and trends addressed in this book.

Fourth, while there is theological and methodological diversity found among the groups addressed in this book, most of them have started with a desire to better contextualize the gospel for a twenty-first-century audience, both in the United States and throughout the world. Developments in missiology regarding the importance of understanding cultures and worldviews, cross-cultural communications, and church planting have influenced these groups to be more engaged in sharing what they believe to be biblical truth within their immediate contexts and throughout the world.

Finally, and closely related to the aforementioned point, these groups developed from a desire to see more people come to faith in Jesus. While it can and should be debated as to whether or not some of these groups have lost this original missionary conviction—and even lack a biblical understanding of the gospel—such discussions are beyond the scope of this book. What is understood from the study of these expressions is that in their origins, there was a desire to see more people enter the kingdom of God.

Throughout this book I have attempted to remain as objective as possible, without providing critique. Since this is a reference book, this approach allows both history and the convictions of such movements to speak for themselves. While there are several expressions in this book in which I am in much agreement, there are others that trouble me to various degrees. My objective is to present the facts and allow those involved in such expressions to speak for themselves.

As with any reference book, the content of this book will provide you with an overview of the topics examined. You will be exposed to definitions, history, common convictions, and individuals who have provided representative leadership for the expression. For those of you interested in further examination of any of the topics of this book, I have concluded each chapter with a short list of resources for additional study. Not only will these provide you with additional depth and insight; they will also contain additional lists of topics and resources for your consideration.

It should also be noted that some of these expressions have already gone through their life cycles, with few people still talking about them. For example, little discussion takes place today in the United States regarding the Church Growth Movement or the Seeker Movement. However, other expressions are just past their births and in the adolescent stages. Here we find Cowboy/Biker/Hip-Hop Churches and the Multisite Church Movement. Regardless of whether or not such expressions are considered passé or current, their influence lives on and they are worthy of being listed in such a reference book. The church stands on the shoulders of those who have gone before us—whether we like it or not.

Throughout this book, I use the terms *trends* and *movements*. I readily admit that such terms are at times used loosely, but not without justification. A trend tends to be a general direction in which something is moving, developing, or progressing, often for at least a decade before it can be labeled a trend. Trends have the potential to make a long-term impact. A movement tends to be more developed than a trend. It often has a clear focus, specific leadership, and complex structures, all related to accomplishing a particular objective. Movements are generally defined as such by both those within and outside the movements.

While my name is on the cover of this book—and I take responsibility for the limitations in its contents—numerous individuals provided me with much assistance in its completion. A special word of appreciation goes to Matt Pierce, my research assistant, who collected numerous articles and books for me. I also had the privilege of working with two secretaries on different occasions while writing this book. So, a thank-you belongs to both Renee Emerson and Amber Walsh.

A big thank-you goes to the people of Thomas Nelson Publishers. It has been a blessing to work with them. I particularly want to thank Heather McMurray and the numerous folks with the company with whom I have been able to work on this project. Their gracious spirit, professionalism, encouragement, flexibility, and willingness to assist in providing such a book to assist individuals and churches was a great blessing.

A word of tremendous appreciation goes to Hannah, Rachel, and Joel Payne, my three wonderful kiddos, and to Sarah, my amazing wife. Thank you, family, for your prayers, encouragement, and patience as I worked on this book.

Above all else, thanksgiving must be given to the Lord. Without him, none of this would have been possible and everything would have been in vain. I committed this book to him before I started writing. It is my hope and prayer that he will use it for the multiplication of disciples, leaders, and churches across the world for his glory.

1

Cell Church Movement

Most churches have some type of small group structure in which Bible study, fellowship, and other activities take place in small groups outside of the larger worship structure. While such gatherings are believed to be very important, most churches would place a higher priority on the corporate worship gathering. If these churches had to choose between having small groups or a large-group worship gathering, they would place priority on the latter. Cell churches, however, have a different philosophy whenever it comes to small groups. While they highly value the corporate worship gathering, they prioritize the small group meeting. Cell churches describe themselves as churches *of* small groups.

Many of the largest churches in the world today are cell churches. Author Ralph W. Neighbour Jr. noted that nineteen out of the twenty largest churches in the world are cell churches,[1] and the Cell Church Movement has caught the attention of media sources such as the *Wall Street Journal* and the *Economist*.[2]

Definition

Cell churches are not affiliated with any one particular denomination or theological perspective and are found across denominational lines. What makes them different is that they hold that the cell is the heart of the church. Pastor Jim Egli provides the following definition of them:

> The definition of a cell church is simple. It is a church that not only meets in a large Sunday gathering but also meets in small groups in homes during the week. The purpose of these cells or home groups is to build up believers in their relationship with Christ and also to reach out and bring others to Christian faith. There is also a goal to raise up future group leaders with the group so that new groups can be formed either by multiplying the initial group into two groups or by planting new groups out of the cell.[3]

History

Proponents of cell churches often cite New Testament passages as examples throughout history for the origins of this model.[4] The modern-day resurgence can be traced back to Korea during the 1960s.[5] Paul Yonggi Cho led his church, Yoido Full Gospel Church, to become a cell church out of desperation. After several years of ministry, Cho arrived at a point of physical exhaustion resulting in hospitalization and a long recuperation process. He did not want to leave his church without a leader during this time. After much time in prayer, studying the Scriptures, and consultation with others, he began to empower and release small group leaders for the ministry.[6]

Cho's model eventually became influential on an international scale. Amor Viviente in Central America began using a home cell paradigm in 1974 followed by Don Robert in the Ivory Coast of Africa in the mid-1970s and Larry Kreider with the Pennsylvanian DOVE Christian Fellowship in the early 1980s.

In the late 1960s and early 1970s, Ralph Neighbour planted a cell church in Houston, Texas. Neighbour would go on to become the strongest advocate of the cell church in the United States. He has trained numerous church leaders from across the globe in cell church methodology, published one of the most significant books on cell churches (*Where Do We Go from Here? A Guidebook for the Cell Group Church*), launched *CellChurch* magazine in 1991, and begun a publishing and training ministry for the cell church model (TOUCH Outreach Ministries).[7]

Bethany World Prayer Center (Baker, Louisiana) became one of the most influential cell churches in the United States by the end of the twentieth century, with more than eight hundred cells and eight thousand people attending Sunday gatherings.[8] Pastor Larry Stockstill of Bethany was influenced by the cell church model of César Castellanos of the International Charismatic Mission (Bogotá, Colombia). Bethany started hosting annual cell church training conferences, and the church has been instrumental in training thousands of pastors in the cell church model.[9]

Within the past few years, several books have been published on cell churches by Joel Comiskey, president and founder of Joel Comiskey Group, a resource ministry for cell churches. These titles include *Myths and Truths of the Cell Church* (2011), *Planting Churches That Reproduce: Starting a Network of Simple Churches* (2008), and *The Church That Multiplies: Growing a Healthy Cell Church in North America* (2007).

Influence

Most of the largest churches in the world are cell churches. In 2000, Joel Comiskey published a list of the ten largest cell churches in the free world (see next page).[10] Within the same article, Comiskey provided a separate list of the three largest "satellite"

Ten Largest Cell Churches

Yoido Full Gospel, Korea
>250,000 in worship attendance
>25,000 cell groups

Grace & Truth, Korea
>105,000 in worship attendance
>Over 1,000 cell groups

Kum Ran Methodist, Korea
>50,000 in worship attendance
>2,700 cell groups

Nambu Full Gospel, Korea
>47,000 in worship attendance
>Number of cell groups unavailable

Elim Christian, El Salvador
>35,000+ in worship attendance
>11,000 cell groups
>120,000 cell attendance

The International Charismatic Mission, Colombia
>35,000+ in worship attendance
>14,000 cell groups
>100,000+ cell attendance

Showers of Grace, Guatemala
>25,000 in worship attendance
>1,000+ cell groups
>15,000 cell attendance

Word of Faith, Kiev, Ukraine

> 20,000 in worship attendance
> Number of cell groups unavailable

Family of God, Indonesia

> 12,000 in worship attendance
> 1000+ cell groups

Faith Community Baptist, Singapore

> 11,000 in worship attendance
> 700 cell groups

(i.e., multisite) cell churches. Though many large cell churches exist in the United States, the record for size belongs to those in other nations. One nation, Korea, has the top four largest cell churches in the world.

Structure

The typical cell church is comprised of two main components, the cell and the celebration service. The cell is most important. There is no definite size to a cell group: they may range from five to fifteen people, or the number that can comfortably gather in the group's small meeting location. Each cell is semiautonomous: the cell often has much freedom in its practices and it does not recognize itself as an individual church but rather a part of the local church. All of the cells together comprise the local church, which is one of the distinctions between a cell church and a house church (see chapter 6). While a house church may be the same size as a cell group—and carry out similar practices—the cell would not define its existence apart from the one local church.

The second component of the cell church is the celebration service. This is the typical weekly corporate worship gathering. During this time all of the cell groups (sometimes in separate worship services) gather for a time of singing, teaching, fellowship, prayer, and other church practices.

Some extremely large cell churches will add a third structure known as the *congregation*. The congregation is a gathering of several regional cell groups. In some churches the congregations will meet in different regions with their cells for weekly worship gatherings. These churches may limit their congregation service to special times of prayer, teaching, or other out-of-the-ordinary meetings.

Practices

The life of the cell church is found in the cell. It is here that accountability, encouragement, and all of the purposes of the church are carried out.

There is no standard set of practices found among cell churches; however, most cell groups will center their weekly activities around biblical teachings, fellowship, prayer, pastoral care, and evangelism. It is common for cells to have a weekly meal together as a part of their gathering and for cell groups to spend time discussing the application of that week's sermon to each member's life. Some cells include worship with songs, communion, and baptisms. Cell groups are known to carry out local community ministries and organize mission trips to other countries. As cells grow, they typically begin other cells by hiving off members for the new groups.

Most cells will have at least one person functioning as the shepherd who provides oversight and care to the group, sometimes with an apprentice who may one day become the leader of a new cell.

> ## Three Largest Satellite Cell Churches
>
> **The Works and Mission Baptist Church, Ivory Coast, Africa**
>
> > 150,000 in worship attendance
> > Hundreds of satellite churches
> > 18,000 cell groups
>
> **Igreja Mana, Lisbon, Portugal**
>
> > 60,000 in worship attendance
> > 400 satellite churches
> > 4,000 cell groups
>
> **New Life Fellowship, Bombay, India**
>
> > 50,000 in worship attendance
> > 250 satellite churches
> > 1,200 cell groups

The leaders of a cell do not understand themselves to be the pastors over the church as a whole. Some churches will designate this person as "pastor," but in many cases the individual is understood to be a cell group leader without a pastoral title. Regardless of the appellation used, the cell church has a typical pyramid-leadership model in place. In addition to leaders found within each cell there are other leaders who oversee several cell group leaders, and additional leaders can be found overseeing the ministry of those leaders just above the cell leaders. At the top of the pyramid is the senior pastor providing oversight to the church. (See diagram on next page.)

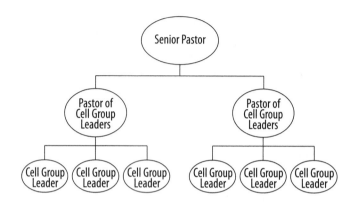

This leadership structure is the second significant distinction between cell churches and house churches (see chapter 6).

Leaders

The people who have been involved in championing the cell church model in the United States have been few in number, but significant in reach. Though many cell churches exist today, and many new churches are embracing cell structures, the number of outspoken advocates for cell churches remains small. Early pioneers from outside the country include David Yonggi Cho from Korea, César Castellanos from Colombia, and Lawrence Khong from Singapore. Some of the significant voices for cell churches from the United States include Ralph W. Neighbour Jr., Joel Comiskey, Carl George, Larry Stockstill, and Larry Kreider.

Notes

1. Ralph W. Neighbour Jr., *Where Do We Go from Here? A Guidebook for the Cell Group Church*, 10th ed. (Houston: Touch Publications, 2000), 37.

2. http://online.wsj.com/article/SB115405424006920089.html; http://www.charismamag.com/index.php/component/content/article/248-people-events/7978-church-growth-strategy-goes-global; http://www.economist.com/node/10015239?story_id=10015239&CFID=25385374.

3. Jim Egli, "A Second Reformation? A History of the Cell Church Movement in the Twentieth Century," *Journal of the American Society for Church Growth* 11 (Winter 2000): 3.

4. William A. Beckham, *The Second Reformation: Reshaping the Church for the Twenty-First Century* (Houston: Touch Publications, 1995); Ralph W. Neighbour Jr., *Where Do We Go from Here*.

5. Egli, "A Second Reformation": 3–16.

6. Cho's story can be found in David Yonggi Cho, *Successful Home Cell Groups* (Gainesville, FL: Bridge-Logos Publishers, 1981).

7. These first three paragraphs of the history of the movement were adapted from Egli, "A Second Reformation": 4–10.

8. Joel Comiskey, *Groups of 12: A New Way to Mobilize Leaders and Multiply Groups in Your Church* (Houston: Touch Publications, 1999), 136.

9. Ibid.

10. Joel Comiskey, "Ten Largest Cell Churches," December 2000, http://www.joelcomiskeygroup.com/articles/worldwide/tenLargest.htm; accessed December 29, 2011.

Additional Resources

Cho, David Yonggi and Harold Hostetler. *Successful Home Cell Groups*. North Brunswick, NJ: Bridge-Logos , 1981.

Comiskey, Joel. *Home Cell Group Explosion: How Your Small Group Can Grow and Multiply*. Houston: Touch Publications, 1998.

———. *Myths and Truths of the Cell Church: Key Principles That Make or Break Cell Ministry*. Moreno Valley, CA: CCS Publishing, 2011.

George, Carl. *Prepare Your Church for the Future*. Grand Rapids: Fleming H. Revell, 1991.

Neighbour, Ralph, Jr. *Where Do We Go from Here? A Guidebook for the Cell Group Church*, 10th ed. (Houston: Touch Publications, 2000).

Stockstill, Larry. *The Cell Church: Preparing Your Church for the Coming Harvest*. Ventura, CA: Regal, 1998.

2

Church Growth Movement

The origins of the contemporary Church Growth Movement date back to 1955 with the publication of the book *The Bridges of God: A Study in the Strategy of Missions* by Donald Anderson McGavran.[1] In this book McGavran argued biblically and historically that the primary way the church has grown has been through people movements—the evangelization and congregationalizing of sizable numbers within a community—as opposed to reaching individuals and extracting them from their communities. He argued that God allowed social networks to develop among the people of the nations of the world (i.e., bridges of God) for the gospel to travel across. And unlike the highly individualized Western contexts, he noted, most of the world's people make significant decisions in light of what their friends and relatives are deciding. To reach individuals without attempting to reach households, tribes, or villages often hindered the advancement of the gospel among a people as unbelieving relatives saw their loved ones being extracted and segregated from the family and friends by the missionaries and their methods.

With the penning of this work, McGavran was soon given the appellation of the father of the movement. Having served as a missionary for many years in India, McGavran was curious as to why some churches grew through the conversion of adults, and other churches did not. McGavran's ideas began to catch on in evangelical circles. He began to conduct research and write about the principles and methods by which churches grow. Interest in McGavran's work became widespread as he began to develop academic courses in church growth and started publishing a periodical on the topic. His writings became widespread, and he became a popular speaker. Over time, more and more church leaders began to desire training in this new discipline known as church growth.

The writings and influence of men such as William Carey, Kenneth Scott Latourette, Roland Allen, and J. Waskom Pickett shaped McGavran's missiology. The movement continued to blossom and develop as he began to use theological, anthropological, and statistical research in answering his question regarding the growth of local churches. In 1965 McGavran was invited to become the founding dean of the School of World Missions at Fuller Theological Seminary, and as a result of his research and Fuller's educational platform, the influence of the Church Growth Movement continued to spread across the globe. By the early 1970s American pastors were seeking McGavran's guidance for the application of church growth principles to their own missiology. In the United States the movement continued to grow throughout the 1970s until the 1990s, eventually spinning off other evangelical expressions, such as the Cell Church Movement, Missional Church Movement, and the Spiritual Warfare Movement, which are detailed in this book.

Definition

The North American Society for Church Growth (currently known as Great Commission Research Network) provides the following as a formal definition of church growth:

> Church growth is that discipline which investigates the nature, expansion, planting, multiplication, function, and health of Christian churches as they relate to the effective implementation of God's commission to "make disciples of all peoples" (Matt. 28:18–20). Students of church growth strive to integrate the eternal theological principles of God's word concerning the expansion of the church with the best insights of contemporary social and behavioral sciences, employing as the initial frame of reference the foundational work done by Donald McGavran.[2]

At the heart of the discipline was the Great Commission to make disciples of the nations. While some writers over the years accused church growth advocates of only being concerned with the numerical growth of local churches, such was not the case. Thom S. Rainer notes, "The heart of church growth is to see those new Christians develop into fruit-bearing disciples of Jesus Christ."[3]

Church growth developed into a field of study alongside other academic disciplines. Scholars accepted it as a legitimate and valuable topic deserving thought, study, and teaching. Bible colleges and seminaries added church growth courses to their catalogs, as well as lectureships in church growth, and professorships. Numerous conferences, books, and seminars developed around the topic as well.

The discipline wed theological and biblical teaching with social sciences and statistics. While these latter two disciplines were not given priority over the theological and biblical foundations, church growth proponents recognized that truth about church health and growth could also be found by applying certain aspects of sociology, anthropology, linguistics, psychology, statistics, and so on when researching how churches are planted, grow, and decline.

McGavran was the leading voice of the movement for almost forty years. As a missionary and missiologist, he was able to develop a foundation for this new discipline that brought together the practical elements of ministry with the academic concepts developed by researchers.

In an attempt to define the movement, Thom S. Rainer offers the following helpful definition: "The Church Growth Movement includes all the resources of people, institutions, and publications dedicated to expounding the concepts and practicing the principles of church growth, beginning with the foundational work of Donald McGavran in 1955."[4]

History

The Church Growth Movement was born outside of the Western world as a result of McGavran's missionary activities in India. During a time when few evangelicals were asking questions regarding the effectiveness of their methods, he began to apply principles of the social sciences to his understanding of missions. His merging of biblical, theological, and social studies resulted in the development of church growth principles that, when applied to the mission field, would serve to plant and grow healthy churches and fulfill the Great Commission. In fact, McGavran argued that "today's paramount task, opportunity, and imperative in missions is to multiply churches in the increasing numbers of receptive peoples of the earth."[5]

After returning to the States in 1961, McGavran opened the Institute of Church Growth at Northwest Christian College in Eugene, Oregon, with the purpose of researching church growth, developing case studies, and teaching church growth to others. In 1965 McGavran moved the institute to Fuller Theological Seminary in Pasadena, California, where he became the founding dean of the School of World Mission. McGavran did not begin teaching church growth classes to North American church leaders until

1972, instead concentrating his attention on those serving in other countries of the world.

There were at least seven major developments in the history of the movement that resulted in Americans learning and applying church growth principles to their context in the United States.[6] The first important milestone was in 1972 when McGavran and C. Peter Wagner co-taught a course in church growth for American church leaders in California. Though this was a pilot class, it made a significant impact on the students. Second was the development of the Institute for American Church Growth. One of the students enrolled in the course, Win Arn, founded this institute in 1972 with four operating purposes:

- To encourage evangelism and church growth in America
- To enable churches to develop strategies and bold plans for growth
- To help churches understand their growth problems and apply principles of church growth to their situations
- To serve as a resource to churches[7]

Through the institute, Arn also developed films and videos, published several books, and taught seminars and workshops related to applying church growth theory to American churches.

Third, in 1973 Arn and McGavran wrote *How to Grow a Church* to introduce Americans to church growth theory and principles. Fourth, in 1976 one of the most influential books related to the spread of church growth in the United States, *Your Church Can Grow: Seven Vital Signs of a Healthy Church* by C. Peter Wagner, was published. In this book Wagner offered readers a biblical perspective on church growth and how they could diagnose their church's health, learn methods of growth from the fastest growing U. S.

congregations, and avoid many growth-related mistakes made by churches.

Fifth, through the leadership of John Wimber and later Carl George, the Charles E. Fuller Institute for Evangelism and Church Growth was initiated. Under Wimber's leadership, the institute became a consulting firm providing expertise in the area of church growth. Sixth, Fuller Theological Seminary developed a doctor of ministry program related to church growth studies. Numerous students completed the program, with many venturing out to develop and lead ministries related to church growth teaching, training, consulting, and resources.

Seventh, the discipline of church growth gained academic and professional credibility. An endowed chair in church growth, the Donald A. McGavran Chair of Church Growth, was provided to Fuller Theologial Seminary in 1984, and C. Peter Wagner was installed as the first incumbent. The development of the American Society for Church Growth and its *Journal of the American Society for Church Growth* provided a professional organization dedicated to networking church growth professors and practitioners.[8] Its annual meetings and journal articles continue to serve as a catalyst for the dissemination of church growth thinking across the United States.

Practices

It was McGavran's research in India in the 1950s that led him to ask a simple yet movement-producing question, "Why do some churches grow and others do not?" This basic question resulted in a movement to discern the barriers to church growth, to devise strategies to overcome such barriers, and to learn from churches that were growing well.

According to George G. Hunter III, the church growth school of thought had at least eight distinctions related to missions and evangelism:

1. The perennial and indispensable work of the mission is apostolic work: continuing the work of the earliest apostles and their congregations in reaching lost people and peoples.
2. The key objective in evangelism is not to "get decisions" but to "make disciples."
3. The key objective in mission is to plant an indigenous evangelizing church among every population.
4. There is no one method for evangelizing or church planting that will fit every population, but the church growth field research approach can help leaders discover the most reproducible methods for reaching any population.
5. The pragmatic test is useful in appraising mission and evangelism strategies and methods allowing churches to employ the approaches that are most effective in the given population.
6. The Christian movement can be advanced by employing the insights and research tools of the behavioral sciences, including the gathering and graphing of relevant statistical data for mission analysis, planning, control, and critique.
7. The Church Growth Movement affirms a high doctrine of the church: the church is Christ's body, all people have the inalienable right to have the opportunity to follow Christ through his body, and the living Christ has promised to build his church.
8. The supreme reason for engaging in evangelism and mission is summarized in Donald McGavran's most famous

declaration: "It is God's will that his church grow, that his lost children be found."[9]

Leaders

McGavran provided not only the foundational work for the birth of the movement but also much of its leadership for several decades until his death in 1990. It can be argued that he was the most influential missiologist of the late twentieth century. Apart from McGavran, C. Peter Wagner has provided enormous support, teaching, and publications related to the movement. As one of the first faculty members of the School of World Mission at Fuller Theological Seminary, Wagner worked very closely with McGavran.

While no other single individual had as much influence as McGavran and Wagner, several others have provided significant leadership in the area of church growth through their teaching, conferences, writings, and ministries. Among those who have had influence in the area of church growth in North America are: Win Arn, Charles Arn, Elmer Towns, John Wimber, Carl George, George Hunter III, Bob Logan, Kent Hunter, Eddie Gibbs, Thom S. Rainer, Gary McIntosh, Lyle Schaller, John Vaughan, Bill Sullivan, George Barna, Charles Van Engen, Eddie Gibbs, and Larry Gilbert.

Notes

1. Donald Anderson McGavran, *The Bridges of God: A Study in the Strategy of Missions* (New York: Friendship Press, 1955).
2. C. Peter Wagner, *Strategies for Church Growth: Tools for Effective Mission and Evangelism* (Ventura, CA: Regal, 1989), 114.
3. Thom S. Rainer, *The Book of Church Growth: History, Theology, and Principles* (Nashville: Broadman and Holman, 1993), 20.
4. Rainer, 22.
5. Donald A. McGavran, *Understanding Church Growth* (Grand Rapids: Eerdmans, 1970), 63.
6. These seven have been adapted from Gary L. McIntosh, ed., *Evaluating the Church Growth Movement: 5 Views* (Grand Rapids: Zondervan,

2004), 16–18.

7. Donald A. McGavran and Winfield C. Arn, *Ten Steps for Church Growth* (San Francisco: Harper and Row, 1977), 13.

8. The society is now known as Great Commission Research Network. The journal is now housed by Biola University in La Mirada, California, and is known as *Great Commission Research Journal*.

9. George G. Hunter III, "The Legacy of Donald A. McGavran," *International Bulletin of Missionary Research* 16, no. 4 (October 1992), 158–59.

Additional Resources

McGavran, Donald A. *The Bridges of God: A Study in the Strategy of Missions.* New York: Friendship Press, 1955.

McIntosh, Gary L. *Biblical Church Growth: How You Can Work with God to Build a Faithful Church.* Grand Rapids, MI: Baker Books, 2003.

———. *Understanding Church Growth.* Grand Rapids: Eerdmans, 1970.

Miles, Delos. *Church Growth: A Mighty River.* Nashville: Broadman, 1981.

Rainer, Thom S. *The Book of Church Growth: History, Theology, and Principles.* Nashville: Broadman and Holman, 1993.

Wagner, C. Peter. *Your Church Can Grow: Seven Vital Signs of a Healthy Church.* Ventura, CA: Regal, 1976.

3

Church-Planting Networks

As observed in the Bible, church planting is evangelism that results in new churches. It is a missionary act whereby new believers are baptized and gathered together to form local churches with their own pastoral leadership. At the turn of the century, evangelicals in the United States began to discuss and participate in church planting with a renewed zeal. While church planting is not new in general, and for evangelicals in particular, what was different was the increased number of individuals, churches, and denominations developing church-planting strategies. While few books existed on the topic of church planting before the twenty-first century, such literature increased during the first decade of the new millennium.

As new churches were being planted in the United States, more and more church planters began to connect with other like-minded leaders, sometimes outside of their denominational affiliations. Such connections were for fellowship, accountability, and learning. Over time, these highly relational, affinity-based connections developed into loose associations of church planters and new churches, with some developing more structure and organization and becoming more formalized into church planting networks.

Definitions

Church Planting. Church planting is the process of starting and developing new local churches. While there are many ways to plant churches the weight of the biblical evidence reveals that it is evangelism that results in new churches. A good example of this can be found in Acts 13–14. As the apostolic teams traveled the world, they would share the gospel, gather new believers together as new churches, and appoint elders for those churches (Acts 14:21–23).

Church-Planting Network. A church-planting network is a group of churches, pastors, and church planters working together to recruit, assess, equip, encourage, and resource church planters.

Development

Church planting networks are not new structures. Throughout history new churches have formed themselves into districts and associations for fellowship, theological accountability, evangelism, missionary activities, and assisting one another with the licensing and ordination of clergy. Some of these connections were loose in structure and organization while others were more formal. The twenty-first-century church saw a rise in church planting networks in the United States for many of the same reasons.

Church-planting networks in the United States can be inter-denominational. Some networks are affiliated with a particular denomination, and sometimes a particular local church, but many networks have members with ties to different denomina-tions. This transdenominational complexion suggests that some church-planting networks are meeting needs that long-standing denominations are failing to address to the satisfaction of their church planters. Regardless of whether or not the network is a part of a denomination or church or comprised of members of different denominations, a few commonalities exist among such networks and reveal the reasons for their growth.

Camaraderie. Church-planting networks tend to function like a band of brothers on a journey together in different geographical locations. Church planting is a unique ministry, one that involves missionary labors. Those who participate in such works are few in number and share a kindred spirit with one another, even if their ministry contexts are physically or theologically distant from one another. Church planters are often in the same stage of life and marriage as other church planters. They are facing similar issues with raising children and financial responsibilities while laboring to plant a church. A new church planter typically has more in common with a church planting pastor of a five-year-old church outside of his denomination than with the senior pastor of a fifty-year-old church within his denomination.

Theological Like-Mindedness. In many denominations theological diversity is not only present but expected. For church planters who are often conservative evangelicals, this broad-mindedness is not helpful and sometimes seen as a distraction from their work. There is a strong appeal to be on a similar page when it comes to matters such as the exclusivity of Jesus' salvation, biblical inerrancy, roles of men and women in the church and home, pastoral leadership, biblical counseling, and so forth. Networks often require a defined set of theological parameters that are sometimes narrower than many denominations.

Relevant Equipping. Since most church planting networks are recent developments, the members of such networks are often at similar stages of development in their ministries. Church planters who have been involved with the network longer than some of the newer members have little difficulty remembering what it was like to begin as a church planter. They can recall with vivid details the challenges they faced raising financial support, locating a meeting place for Sunday gatherings, and learning how to preach. Because of the closeness of the stages of ministry development it is easy for the more experienced church planters to provide assessment, coaching, mentoring, training, and practical guidance to those who are close behind them in the church planting process. Those within networks have similar needs, interests, and passions. As a result of these commonalities, most networks are able to provide timely and relevant assistance to their church planters. In contrast, individual denominations have church leaders at different stages of ministry development and therefore some denominational resources are irrelevant to church planters.

Specific Missional Focus. In many denominations missions refers to many activities outside of church planting in which the church participates (e.g., teaching children, medical missions, crusades). Church planting networks offer a focus on mission in terms of evangelism and church planting. This specificity helps rally church planters together around the cause of church planting. Rather than diversifying their missionary activities, church planting networks concentrate attention on a specific Great Commission activity.

Leaders

There are dozens of church planting networks within the United States. The following is an overview of a few of the networks in the United States along with information from their websites.

Acts 29. "The Mission of Acts 29 is to band together Christian, Evangelical, Missional & Reformed churches, who, for the sake of Jesus and the gospel, plant new churches and replant dead and dying churches across the United States and the world. This work is done in obedience to the great commission (Matt. 28:18–20), with the goal of seeing millions of lives changed by the power of the gospel. Acts 29 network exists to build a unifying and an uncommon alliance of smaller networks to advance the mission of Jesus through church planting churches. We are planting churches that are missionaries in their respective communities sent by Jesus with the gospel (John 20:21). It is our commitment to focus our efforts on planting multiplying churches and training leaders."[1]

Church Multiplication Associates. "Church Multiplication Associates (CMA) is a growing and emerging family of churches intent on being alive with Jesus, mutually encouraging and spontaneously reproductive. We are not a denomination but in fact have churches that represent many denominations. CMA is not a network of churches either, but a voluntary association of a multiplicity of expanding networks.[2] Church Multiplication Associates (CMA) exists to facilitate church multiplication movements by focusing resources on reproducing healthy disciples, leaders, churches and movements. We pursue the fulfillment of mission with the following four objectives . . . (1) To be a catalyst for a church multiplication vision among churches . . . (2) To focus resources toward the reproduction of healthy churches. (3) To assist in developing, assessing and deploying leaders for new churches and regional movements. (4) To function in partnership with other like ministries in God's kingdom for the fulfillment of the Great Commission."[3]

Glocalnet. Glocalnet is the church planting arm with Northwood Church in Keller, Texas. "Glocalnet was born out of a dream—a dream that followers of Jesus Christ and their churches would be so radically changed from the inside out that those disciples, their families, their churches, their neighborhoods, and their work places would never be the same. And as a result of a transformational experience, these disciples and their churches would form partnerships that would transform their communities and touch the world. Groups of regionally-located churches or churches within the same city (clusters of churches) would link arms to provide cities and nations good news in all arenas—fresh water, nutritional food, 21st century healthcare, competitive education, and spiritual truth. If this worldwide, strategic, interdenominational alliance of churches went full-force after its calling from Christ to be salt and light to serve the least of these glocally (locally and globally), the world would literally be transformed. Every pocket of the globe would be changed."[4]

Orchard Group. "The churches started by the Orchard Group identify with the Christian Church Movement ... Starting new churches is the best way to reach new residents, new people groups and new generations with the gospel. Orchard Group has been planting churches in the New York City metropolitan area for over sixty years and in the rest of the northeastern United States for twenty years. New churches started by Orchard Group since 2000 are reaching over a thousand people in the metro areas of Boston, New York, Philadelphia, Baltimore, Washington and Pittsburgh. In the past few years we have expanded to other challenging, strategic, urban settings: Salt Lake City, Central Phoenix, Ventura, CA and Limerick, Ireland. While we anticipate starting more churches in other U.S. and international cities, our highest priorities continue to be New York and the northeast."[5]

Redeemer City to City. Redeemer City to City developed from the ministry of Redeemer Presbyterian Church in New York City. "Our mission is to help leaders build gospel movements in cities[6] ... We are dedicated to training leaders and planting churches that are committed to strengthening the influence of the gospel in the city in ways that result in spiritual growth, the flourishing of neighborhoods, reconciliation between classes and races, and the renewal of family life, education, health, and vocation ... Redeemer City to City is drawing on what we have learned in New York City and other global cities over the past twenty years collaborating with a growing number of church planters and leaders around the world. We help recruit, train, coach and fund national church planters working in transdenominational church planting networks in more than 60 global cities, with the hope of seeing these networks multiply churches, become self-sustaining and bring the gospel to bear on their city."[7]

Sovereign Grace. "Sovereign Grace Ministries was founded in 1982 out of Covenant Life Church in Gaithersburg, Maryland[8] ... Our church-planting process is designed to set church planters up for success. We try to think about that success not in terms of five-year plans, but in terms of 50 years. We want to have something meaningful to hand over to the next generation. Gospel success means gospel transfer—that the good news of Jesus Christ would be shared with the members of every church plant, and with the generations to come."[9]

Stadia. "Stadia brings people and churches together to transform lives and communities through church planting. Together with our networks, we plant high potential churches by sharing resources, best practices and support. Together with our planters, we create the healthiest church-planting environment possible by providing the best planter and spousal care, coaching and project management. Together with our donors, we invest vital resources into new churches to transform lives and communities."[10]

Future

The number of church planting networks continues to grow. Church planters, weary from denominational politics, perceived irrelevance, squabbles over theological minutiae, lack of evangelistic zeal, and perceived waste of financial resources are continuing to devote more and more of their time and zeal to church-planting networks. Interdenominational (across denomination) networks are likely to grow at a much faster rate than intradenominational (within denomination) networks. Denominational leaders are recognizing that many of their younger and better leaders are connecting to both the denominational and the network structures. This dual allegiance has caused concern among many within denominations, and while some leaders have reacted negatively, some have been supportive and others are developing church planting networks within their denominational networks to fill the niche. A report from the Leadership Network noted that "the energy of successful church planting seems to be moving quickly from denominational structures to hands-on local churches and networks."[11]

Notes

1. http://www.acts29network.org/about/vision/; accessed December 13, 2011.
2. http://www.cmaresources.org/about; accessed December 13, 2011.
3. http://www.cmaresources.org/about/mission_values; accessed December 13.
4. http://www.glocal.net/dna/; accessed December 28, 2011.
5. http://www.orchardgroup.org/#/about; accessed December 28, 2011.
6. http://redeemercitytocity.com/our-story.jsp; accessed May 29, 2012.
7. http://redeemercitytocity.com/our-story/approach.jsp; accessed December 28, 2011.
8. http://www.sovereigngraceministries.org/about-us/default.aspx.
9. http://www.sovereigngraceministries.org/church-planting/plant-with-us/how-we-plant-churches.aspx.
10. http://www.stadia.cc/?page_id=7; accessed December 28, 2011.
11. Ed Stetzer and Dave Travis, "Church Planting Overview: State of Church Planting USA," Leadership Network, 2007, 4; free download available at http://leadnet.org/resources/download/church_planting_overview_state_of_church_planting_usa; accessed December 13, 2011.

Additional Resources

Few resources exist to date on church-planting networks. The best resources are the websites of the networks themselves.

Brown, Sherri. "Creating Strategic Alliances and Partnerships for Planting New Churches," Leadership Network, 2007; http://leadnet.org/resources/download/creating_strategic_alliances_and_partnerships_for_planting_new_churche/.

Stetzer, Ed and Dave Travis, "Church Planting Overview: State of Church Planting in the USA," Leadership Network, 2007; http://leadnet.org/resources/download/church_planting_overview_state_of_church_planting_usa; accessed 12/28/2011.

Stetzer, Ed and David Putman, "Emerging Networks: New Paradigms of Partnership," in *Breaking the Missional Code: Your Church Can Become a Missionary in Your Community*. Nashville, TN: Broadman and Holman Publishers, 2006, 170–79.

Stetzer, Ed and Warren Bird, "New Players: Aggressive Local Church and Church Planting Networks," in *Viral Churches: Helping Church Planters Become Movement Makers*. San Francisco, CA: Jossey-Bass, 2010, 49–65

Williams, Andy. "Church Multiplication Centers: Best Practices from Churches That Do High-Yield Church Planting," Leadership Network, 2005; http://leadnet.org/resources/download/church_multiplication_centers/.

Woodley, Matt. "A Calling Confirmed," *Leadership Journal* (Fall 2010): 25–28.

4

Cowboy / Biker / Hip-Hop Churches

While there is a long history of churches existing among different ethnic groups in the United States (e.g., Chinese, Korean, African-American), the church has recently observed the growth of new churches among individual subcultures and affinity groups. Three of the more common expressions to date have been among cowboys, bikers, and the hip-hop communities. While the number of cowboy churches is the fastest growing and most numerous of the three, it is likely that the numbers among the latter two will increase in the future.

Various churches have become seeker friendly to these particular demographics in an attempt to reach these communities. The worship gatherings are designed as places for people to "come as you are." These weekly gatherings, small groups, and leadership training systems in the churches attempt to reflect several of the cultural elements of the subcultures as they are appropriate. Their approaches to contextualization help take the gospel to these communities in their own settings.

Cowboy Churches

The majority of the writings available on cowboy churches exist online and as broadcast stories from local and national news stations. [1] It is difficult to estimate the number of such churches in the United States, but according to Barbara Bedrick cowboy churches are listed in twenty-nine states.[2] A search of the American churches listed in the directory located at www.cowboychurch.net reveals several hundred results, but it should be noted that some of these groups are ministries and not exclusively local churches. The Cowboy Church Network of North America, which is a Southern Baptist-affiliated network, lists 58 churches.[3] The American Fellowship of Cowboy Churches identifies 204 churches in their network.[4] And the International Cowboy Church Alliance Network estimates between 600 and 800 such churches exist in the United States.[5]

Many of these churches would be quick to explain that they are more focused on reaching the "Western Heritage" subculture rather than simply cowboys. The Nazarene Cowboy Church Network identifies seven such categories of the Western heritage demographic:

1. Working cowboys make all or part of their living on horseback. They represent a small part of this population and they may be the hardest to reach.
2. Professional rodeo cowboys make all or a part of their living on the rodeo circuit and again are very few in number.
3. Arena cowboys and cowgirls make their living somewhere other than the ranch or rodeo, but they participate in arena activities such as team roping, barrel racing, team penning, ranch rodeo, sorting, cutting, play day, and so on.
4. Cattle people may be large ranchers with hundreds or

thousands of heads of cattle or people who own a few cows or even one FFA steer. They may or may not use horses.

5. Horse people are people who love horses. They may trail ride or western pleasure ride, show horses, raise horses, race horses, or just have a few nags in the pasture—and they may or may not care anything about a cow.

6. Cowboys at heart are people who just love the cowboy and what he stands for. They wear boots, jeans, and a cowboy hat; they listen to country music; have all of John Wayne's movies on DVD; and Captain Augustus McCrae and Captain Woodrow F. Call are their heroes.

7. Cowboy-mentality people may be linked to the culture through their past, parents, or family. They are people who live by a code: your word is your bond and an honest day's work for an honest day's pay. They may be electricians, carpenters, law enforcement officers, firefighters, businesspeople, working folks, country folks, people who love the land, farmers, hunters, and fishermen. You could even include anyone who has ever watched a western.[6]

As a recent trend, evangelicals began to witness the birth of cowboy churches in the 1980s.[7] While the average size of such churches is two hundred people,[8] Cowboy Church of Ellis County (Waxahachie, Texas) notes that from twelve hundred to fifteen hundred people attend their weekly worship services, making the church "the largest Cowboy Church in the world."[9] These churches represent different denominations or are not affiliated with any denominational affiliation. It is normative for such churches to meet in barns, stables, rodeo arenas, or other common gathering areas for those who are part of the western heritage subculture.

Worship gatherings are very simple and laid-back in nature. A "come-as-you-are" expectation is typical, with people's dress usually consisting of blue jeans, cowboy boots, and cowboy hats. Music tends to be of the country, western, or bluegrass genre. The pastor tends to preach without notes but with a Bible in his hand. In some instances, offerings are collected by passing around a cowboy hat for an offering plate. Baptisms are normally done in horse watering troughs.

Leaders of cowboy churches cite the Great Commission, to go out and make disciples of the nations, as the motive behind the planting of such churches. According to Ron Nolen, a consultant with the Baptist General Convention of Texas, "When we send people overseas as missionaries, we tell them to spend time learning the culture so they can understand the people they're ministering to. That's just as important when dealing with cowboys."[10] Many cowboy church leaders decide to start churches because they believe that conventional churches are not reaching people in the cowboy subculture. For example, Perry Smith, pastor of Living for the Brand Cowboy Church (Athens, Texas), commented, "Our goal is to take down any barriers that would prevent someone from finding God."[11] Charles Higgs, director of Texas Baptists' western-heritage ministry, said: "About 10 percent of the 25 million people in Texas relate to western-heritage culture ... Many factors keep these people from feeling comfortable in traditional churches, from the music to style of dress. Cowboy churches have built bridges for this unreached group by integrating culture and church."[12] Higgs noted the evangelistic effectiveness of such churches in his state: "The average Texas Baptist church baptizes 10 people per year ... Western-heritage churches baptize 26 per year. Eighty percent of our [cowboy church] baptisms are adults. Eighty percent of those adults are men."[13]

While the point has been raised that such churches are only for the western heritage demographic, church leaders are quick to disagree. Many pastors share the same conviction as Wally Varnell, pastor of Cleveland Cowboy Church (Cleveland, Tennessee): "You don't need to be a cowboy or from the country to attend ... Not everyone who comes owns a tractor, horses or cattle, but we all realize our human need for fellowship with God. So, whether you have a Harley or a horse, wear boots or suits, it just doesn't matter. Cowboy Church is a place you can feel welcome and right at home."[14]

Biker Churches

While not as numerous as cowboy churches, biker churches have been springing up across the United States in the past decade. These churches grew out of a deep conviction to share the gospel with those in the biker subculture. Freedom Biker Church is one such example. According to the church's website, their history is rooted in a Great Commission vision.

It is common to read of such churches advertising that Sunday worship attire includes leather, tattoos, and jeans. Biker churches are similar to cowboy churches, providing a worship gathering for anyone; a "come as you are" welcome. For example, Crossfire United Methodist Church advertises: "We know that many don't feel comfortable in the 'traditional church' setting so we are making a place where long

> ### Freedom Biker Church
>
> Our Story began with a real passion to introduce bikers to Jesus Christ, and provide them with a real place to grow into committed followers of Him. Not simply to introduce them to church, but to Jesus! For us, the ministry of Freedom Biker Church represents a place of belonging for those who come. We have worked hard to create a church culture that is relevant to the motorcycle community. A place where folks can grow spiritually in a natural way.[15]

hair, shaved heads, beards, tattoos, skate boarders, bikes, and Rock and Roll are common. Crossfire was started by bikers for bikers but, all are welcome here, come as you are!"[16] The Biker Church (Boyertow, Pennsylvania) is very clear with their mission: "To love and accept the unchurched biker where he or she is. To demonstrate to them Christ's likeness in action. [To] display compassion while resisting the temptations to give solutions, but instead listen with love. [To] create a place of safety where they can freely bare their soul and receive love, ministry and healing through the power of the Holy Spirit."[17]

Paul White, founder and pastor of Salvation Saloon (Clearwater, Florida), was aware of the cultural differences between many established churches and the biker community. This was one of his reasons for planting Salvation Saloon. White said, "If they [bikers] weren't going to go to a traditional church, then we felt like, well, we'll take it to them."[18]

With events such as "Bring a Heathen to Church Month," the church connects with an edgy and tough crowd. Salvation Saloon was planted in 2006 and within two years had a congregation composed of 60 percent bikers and 40 percent non-bikers. At the time of this writing, the church meets in a comedy club, the music is of the rock and blues genres, the sermon is delivered from a bar stool, and the offering is collected in a motorcycle helmet that is passed among the people.[19]

As with the cowboy churches, biker churches recognized that many within their subculture would not feel very comfortable in a traditional church setting and are proactive in embracing bikers.

Biker Church

This is not an organization, club or association but a Church where you can come and "feel right at home," among peers and friends who have a love for Christ. Most of us on staff have been involved in motorcycles and the life for years and know how hard sometimes it is to "fit in" among those who don't understand our lives. The Biker Church Does! It is Bikers ministering with Bikers. This church welcomes all no matter what Club, Organization, or Patch you might be a part of or wear.[20]

While the number of biker churches is not known, a Google search reveals the popularity. The Biker Friendly Church Network lists eighty-nine "biker-friendly" churches, churches who are sympathetic to the biker subculture, in twenty-two states.[21]

Hip-Hop Churches

The origins of the hip-hop subculture can be traced back to the 1970s and include music, graffiti art, and dance. What began in the Bronx, New York, as a response to post-industrializational urban social problems quickly developed into a subculture of its own that has not only spread across the United States but into other countries as well. While hip-hop is often equated with the African-American community or a musical genre, the term is much broader. Daniel White Hodge described it as "larger than the radio, larger than commercialized artists, larger than record industry branding. It is a culture, a people, a movement, a growing community of people that live, breathe, eat, love, hate and work just as anyone else does. Hip-hop cannot be easily understood or defined. It is complex and full of narratives that would blow away even the strongest anthropologist."[22]

Hodge has defined hip-hop as "an urban subculture that seeks to express a lifestyle, attitude or theology. Rejecting the dominant culture, it seeks to increase social consciousness, cultural awareness and racial pride. Rap music functions as the vehicle by which the cultural messages of Hip Hop are sent, and the industry by which Hip Hop culture is funded and propagated."[23]

As the Hip-Hop Movement continued to grow and flourish, evangelical Christians began to engage those within the subculture with the gospel and plant churches among them. While there were churches that developed ministries and sought to use elements of the subculture for evangelism, discipleship, and worship services before it, Crossover Community Church (Tampa, Florida), founded in 2000, is considered the first true hip-hop church.[24]

Urban Jerusalem (aka Urban J), another hip-hop church, was started in Minneapolis in 2006 by Stacey and Tryenyse Jones as a way to reach younger adults. According to Stacey, "We're trying to tap into the Gen X and millennial generation that hunger [sic] for more spirituality but doesn't feel comfortable in a regular church.... Studies have shown that they are, by a wide margin, the most unchurched generation. We need something to grab their attention. Our vision is to present God in a relevant form, and for many young people, that means music."[25]

Efrem Smith, author of The Hip-Hop Church, shares the reason for starting such churches: "We really have to work to help people understand that we are not doing this for the cool factor but truly in order to advance God's kingdom among urban, un-churched youth and young adults. You really have to be prayed up and strategic in your use of hip-hop ministry models. These models must be connected to your vision, mission, and core values. At the end of the day, hip-hop has to be more than a Sunday worship experience; it has to be a part of a larger congregational vision of evangelism, discipleship, and missions."[26]

Ralph C. Watkins offers an assessment of what is needed in order to reach the hip-hop generation. He notes that while the church should engage the people in their contexts, the church is not to become a club or avoid that which contains spiritual truth. "Churches that will be effective in evangelizing the hip hop generation will be churches that are somewhat radical while at the same time not being too radical," he said. "This means that the church's being radical and relevant must be held in tension with the church's bearing some resemblance to the old church. Hip hoppers want their cake, and they believe they can eat it too. They want the ministry to be cutting edge by trying new and relevant things that look nonreligious but have a spiritual appeal.... This is a tough walk, but each church must be led by God and its pastor as to how God is calling it to negotiate this balance."[27]

An official number of hip-hop churches in the United States isn't available; however, at the time of this writing, their numbers appear to be small. What tends to be more commonplace is traditional churches beginning a periodic worship gathering—or other regular special event—including art, dance, music, dress, and communication styles that are designed to connect with hip-hop communities in order to share the gospel.

The following churches have designated themselves as hip-hop churches:

- The House Covenant Church (Chicago)
- Crossover Church (Tampa, Florida)
- Street Life (Houston, Texas)
- Hip-Hop Sanctuary New Generation Church (Moreno Valley, California)
- Urban Jerusalem (Minneapolis, Minnesota)
- New City (Cleveland, Ohio)
- Christ Crucified Fellowship (New York)

Commonalities

While the births and growth of cowboy, biker, and hip-hop churches are a recent trend among three different segments of American society, there are at least four missiological commonalities between them. These similarities reveal the influence of other movements and trends (i.e., church planting networks, Missional Church Movement, Seeker Movement: see chapters 3, 9, 12).

Attractional Approach. Often those planting and serving such churches want to create a place where unbelievers can "come as they are" to hear the gospel—this environment is generally the weekly worship gathering. Wherever the gathering is held, a way is sought to attract unbelievers to a context where they will be welcomed and not shunned. Recognizing that many people within such subcultures have been turned off by more conventional churches, these new expressions strive to share the gospel within their own contexts.

Contextualization. Cowboy, biker, and hip-hop churches labor diligently to overcome the cultural barriers that exist between unbelievers and the gospel message. Church leaders attempt to think like missionaries and work to discard the preconceived and stereotypical cultural expectations that most people have about conventional churches. The music, language, dress, demeanor, and aesthetics mirror those of the subculture rather than those of the typical mainstream churches. For example, the podium behind which the preacher stands might be constructed out of the handlebars of a motorcycle. The call to worship could be the revving of a Harley's engine or the parading of the American and Christian flags by individuals riding into the worship area on horseback. Such churches welcome boots, leather, denim, hats, and baggy pants, and make it very explicit that such dress is not unusual.

Newly Planted Churches. These churches are a recent development. The original pastors of many of these churches are still active.

Evangelism and Church-Planting Emphases. It is rare to hear of such churches being started without evangelistic zeal driving the founders. These new expressions come about as a result of leaders recognizing that many people within American subcultures are not being reached with the gospel. Closely related to this passion for evangelism is a strong desire to plant other churches. Networks exist to link these churches together and help facilitate church planting. Some examples include the Cowboy Church Network of North America and the Biker Friendly Church Network.

Notes

1. For a few examples of local and national television coverage on cowboy churches see: http://www.youtube.com/watch?v=xvPLQ5qNLlI; http://www.youtube.com/watch?v=4f2QnFb_IxA; http://www.youtube.com/watch?v=5A1GCbtUV9Y; http://www.kten.com/story/16223568/local-cowboy-church-braves-cold-to-make-christmas-merry; http://www.myfoxdfw.com/dpp/news/fox_4_features/lone_star/cowboy-church-ropes-them-in; accessed January 2, 2012.

2. Barbara Bedrick, "Cowboy Church Appeal Spreading Thanks to Laid-back Approach," *Associated Baptist Press*, January 17, 2007; http://www.abpnews.com/archives/item/1732-cowboy-church-appeal-spreading-thanks-to-laid-back-approach.

3. http://www.cowboycn.org/; accessed October 4, 2011.

4. http://www.americanfcc.org/content.cfm?id=213&content_id=206; accessed October 4, 2011.

5. http://iccanlink.ning.com/; accessed October 6, 2011. E-mail to author from Edward Starks, Education Director for ICCAN and Round Pen Bible Institute, received October 4, 2011.

6. http://www.dallasnaz.org/images/5274/pdf/Nazarene%20Cowboy%20Church%20Network.pdf; accessed October 4, 2011.

7. Michelle Bearden, "Cowboy Church Blends Gospel, Horse Training," *Tampa Bay Online*; http://www2.tbo.com/lifestyles/life/2010/jul/15/cowboy-church-blends-gospel-horse-training-ar-47026//.

8. Bedrick, "Cowboy Church Appeal Spreading."

9. http://www.cowboychurchoffelliscounty.org/about-us/welcome/; accessed October 6, 2011.

10. Linda Owen, "Worship at the O.K. Corral," *Christianity Today* 47, no. 9 (September 2003): 63.

11. Art Lawler, "Cowboy Church to Celebrate 10 Years," *Athens Review*, July 15, 2010, http://www.athensreview.com/local/x961152036/Cowboy-church-to-celebrate-10-years/print.

12. Lauren Hollon, "Cowboy Church Rounds Up Strays in Brenham," *Baptist Standard*, July 21, 2010; http://www.baptiststandard.com/index.php?option=com_content&task=view&id=11411&Itemid=53.

13. Ibid.

14. "Cleveland Now Has a Cowboy Church," *Cleveland Daily Banner,* June 6, 2010; http://www.clevelandbanner.com/view/full_story/7900243 /article-Cleveland-now-has-a-Cowboy-Church.

15. http://freedombikerchurch.com/about-us/our-story/; accessed October 6, 2011.

16. http://www.bikerchurch.com/main/default.htm; accessed October 6, 2011.

17. http://www.thebikerchurchpa.com/; accessed October 6, 2011.

18. Ann Marie Hughes, "Leather and Grace: A Biker Church Thrives," *St. Petersburg Times,* October 5, 2008; http://www.tampabay.com/news /humaninterest/article837808.ece.

19. Ibid.

20. http://www.thebikerchurch.org/main.html; accessed October 6, 2011.

21. http://www.bikerfriendlychurchnetwork.org/find.php; accessed October 6, 2011.

22. Daniel While Hodge, *The Soul of Hip Hop: Rims, Timbs and a Cultural Theology* (Downers Grove, IL: IVP 2010), 20.

23. Ibid., 38.

24. Efrem Smith and Phil Jackson, *The Hip-Hop Church: Connecting with the Movement Shaping Our Culture* (Downers Grove, IL: IVP 2005), 145.

25. Jeff Strickler, "Hip-Hop Church Rocks the Message," *News Observer.com,* April 8, 2011; http://www.newsobserver.com/2010/04/08/426519 /hip-hop-church-rocks-the-message.html.

26. Robert Gelinas, "Bringing Hip-Hop to Church," March 10, 2009; http://www.urbanfaith.com/2009/03/bringing-hip-hop-to-church .html/; accessed October 7, 2011.

27. Ralph C. Watkins, *The Gospel Remix: Reaching the Hip Hop Generation* (Valley Forge, PA: Judson 2007), 67.

Additional Resources

Cowboy Churches

Bedrick, Barbara, "Cowboy Church Appeal Spreading Thanks to Laid-Back Approach," *Associated Baptist Press,* January 16, 2007, (online) http://www .abpnews.com/content/view/1732/120/.

Grossman, Cathy Lynn, "Cowboy Church Rounds 'em Up on Sunday," *USA Today*; March 11, 2003, (online) http://www.usatoday.com/life/2003-03-10 -cowboy-church-usat_x.htm.

Owen, Linda. "Worship at the O.K. Corral: Cowboy Churches Shape Their Ministries for the Western at Heart," *Christianity Today* 47, no. 9, (September 2003): 62–64.

Hip-Hop Churches

Hodge, Daniel White. *The Soul of Hip Hop: Rims, Timbs and a Cultural Theology*. Downers Grove, IL: IVP Books, 2010.

Smith, Efrem, and Phil Jackson, *The Hip-Hop Church: Connecting with the Movement Shaping Our Culture*. Downers Grove, IL: IVP, 2005.

Watkins, Ralph C. *The Gospel Remix: Reaching the Hip Hop Generation*. Valley Forge, PA: Judson, 2007.

Biker Churches

David, Gary. "Biker Church Is Where Jesus Can 'Clean You Up on the Inside,'" *Baptist Press*, April 12, 2000, (online) http://www.bpnews.net/bpnews .asp?id=5626.

Hughes, Ann Marie. "Leather and Grace: A Biker Church Thrives," *Tampa Bay Times*, October 5, 2008, (online) http://www.tampabay.com/news/humaninterest /article837808.ece.

WSLS News Staff. "Biker Church Roanoke Hold First Service," July 22, 2010, (online) http://www2.wsls.com/news/2010/jul/22 /first_biker_church_service-ar-359898/.

5

Emerging Church Movement

Scot McKnight has referred to the Emerging Church Movement as "one of the most controversial and misunderstood movements today."[1] While this movement has extensive connections beyond North America, discussions among evangelicals began to develop in the 1990s regarding how to effectively engage postmodernism in the United States. These discussions led to the development of the Emerging Church Movement.

Recognizing that significant cultural shifts were occurring in North America around this time, evangelicals started asking how the church should respond with the gospel. Those within the movement believed that a healthy critique of the modern church was necessary to show that the church needed to emerge from an older paradigm and become more representative of Christendom. Within a short period of time, however, the movement began to fragment over the matter of epistemology, hermeneutics, and, ultimately, theology. Those who were theologically more conservative became known as the "emerging church," while the more theologically moderate and liberal group became known as "Emergent" (called "emergent church" by some). Both groups remain under the broad umbrella appellation "Emerging Church Movement." What began as a missional movement to engage postmodern paradigms with the gospel and assimilate them into local churches became two distinct, yet often misunderstood, groups that viewed the gospel, church, and mission from radically different perspectives.

Definitions

Mark Driscoll was one of the first people to identify with the movement in the 1990s. While describing his engagement with and ultimate separation from the developing Emergent group, Driscoll offered the following as a definition of the movement:

> The emerging church is a growing, loosely connected movement of primarily young pastors who are glad to see the end of modernity and are seeking to function as missionaries who bring the gospel of Jesus Christ to emerging and postmodern cultures. The emerging church welcomes the tension of holding in one closed hand the unchanging truth of evangelical Christian theology (Jude 3) and holding in one open hand the many cultural ways of showing and speaking Christian truth as a missionary to America (1 Cor. 9:19–23).[2]

Emergent leader Tony Jones acknowledged that it is very difficult to define the Emergent Movement. In his book, *The New Christians*, he explains the difficulties he encountered and the priority given to relationships over doctrine or practices:

> In the end, what makes the emergents difficult to define is the relational nature of the movement. Whereas traditional groupings of Christians are either bounded sets (for example, Roman Catholicism or Presbyterianism—you know whether you're in or out based on membership) or centered sets (for example, evangelicalism, which centers on certain core beliefs), emergent Christians do not have membership or doctrine to hold them together. The glue is relationship. That makes it difficult to put one's finger on

just what emergent is; to the question "What do you all hold in common?" the answer is most likely "We're friends."[3]

To provide some clarity, Jones shared the following definitions common to the emergent church discussions.[4]

- **Emergent**. Usually used with a capital "E" to refer to a network formed in 1997. Emergent is also short for Emergent Village (www.emergentvillage.org).

- **Emergents**. Adherents of emergent Christianity.

- **Emergent Christianity**. New forms of the Christian faith as understood and practiced by the emergents.

- **Emergent Church**. New forms of church life found in America beginning in the twentieth century, coming from modernity. The terms "emergent" and "emerging" are often used interchangeably.

Practices

In their book *Emerging Churches: Creating Christian Community in Postmodern Cultures*, Eddie Gibbs and Ryan K. Bolger define emerging churches as "communities that practice the way of Jesus within postmodern cultures." For them, nine practices are involved in this way: Emerging churches (1) identify with the life of Jesus, (2) transform the secular realm, and (3) live highly communal lives. Because of these three activities, they (4) welcome the stranger, (5) serve with generosity, (6) participate as producers, (7) create as created beings, (8) lead as a body, and (9) take part in spiritual activities.[5]

When churches identify with Jesus, they grasp the gospel and participate in the mission of God in the world. Such churches attempt to remove the sacred and secular barrier. They desire a holistic spirituality and are ready to discard any trappings of modernity that detract from the gospel. Emerging churches focus on living life together rather than placing the focus on service. They work to form tight communities, believing that church is a people. Rather than argue about faith, emerging churches seek to welcome, listen, and learn from those of other faith traditions. They desire to love all people without targeting them. Emerging churches serve their communities with the expectation of nothing in return. As the emerging church gathers for worship, they seek to produce expressions that are reflective of who they are. These churches express themselves in worship in a variety of creative ways. Church leaders work to serve without embracing any domineering and controlling leadership expressions. Such churches are comfortable experimenting with ancient spiritual expressions from church history in conjunction with more modern and normative spiritual disciplines.

Beliefs

The diversity of the movement poses a challenge when attempting to provide a summary of any common beliefs. However, Scot McKnight has identified five themes that characterize the Emerging Church Movement. According to McKnight, all of these "streams" flow together into one large "emerging lake."[6]

Prophetic (or Provocative) Rhetoric. The church needs to work to be intentionally provocative by drawing attention to their concerns.

Postmodern. Postmodernism was a rejection of many of the foundations on which the Enlightenment was built. Postmodern philosophers advocated that "there is no one meaning of the world, no transcendent center to reality as a whole."[7] Under postmodernity, truth became subjectively constructed by societies at different times in history, with no one grand metanarrative to be applied to all peoples at all times. Some within the Postmodern Movement have intentionally chosen to minister to and with postmodern people. However, others within the movement have decided to minister as postmoderns.

Those within this latter category often question the Bible, absolute/propositional truth, the exclusivity of salvation in Jesus, and other convictions that have existed for the two thousand years of church history. They draw the most attention with their writings and presentations—and create the most conflict. It is common for them to embrace postmodern ways of thought, such as rejecting metanarratives, and subscribe to the social construction of relativistic truth. These postmodernists are more likely to consider themselves as part of Emergent.

Praxis-Oriented. Emergents are concerned about how the faith is lived out in the real world. This includes concerns regarding proper worship expressions, Christian lifestyles, social ministry, and missions.

Post-Evangelical. The Emergent Movement grew as a response to evangelicalism. While the majority of the members of the movement are evangelical in their theology, this post-evangelical label is appropriate for two-reasons: (1) they tend to be suspicious of systematic theology, believing that God revealed a narrative about himself and no single systematic theology is capable of capturing and explaining God fully; and (2) conversations—even among some of those who believe that Jesus is the only way of salvation—about those who are in the kingdom of God and those who are out of the kingdom of God frustrate and encourage skepticism. The use of language about who is "in" and who is "out" is not viewed with favor among post-evangelical emergent churches.

Political. Many within the movement lean toward the left when it comes to politics, which is a shift away from traditional conservative evangelical belief. Many emergent churches are strongly engaged with social activism and social ministries.

History[8]

Within the United States the origins of the Emerging Church Movement date back to the 1990s. In 1997, the Leadership Network of Dallas, Texas, brought together a dozen young leaders to begin discussing ministry to Generation X (those born between 1961 and 1981). Over the next three years, a series of conversations and relationships developed that would result in the Emergent Movement. By 1999 conflict arose in the group over theological convictions that resulted in fragmentation. When the year 2000 arrived, the relationship between these leaders and the relationship with the sponsoring Leadership Network was falling apart, and an organization known as Emergent was created in 2001. Shortly after the separation from Leadership Network, Emergent partnered with Youth Specialties to publish books and sponsor events. An Emergent Convention was then attached to the National Pastors' Convention that Youth Specialties hosts annually.

Numerous conferences have been held supporting both the Emergent and emerging perspectives, and a large number of books have been published by authors representing both sides, as well as articles and blog posts offering their critiques of both sides.

Leaders

Influential leaders with Emergent include Tony Jones, Doug Pagitt, Brian McLaren, Mark Oestreicher, Karen Ward, Chris Seay, and Ivy Beckwith. Those involved with the Emerging Church Movement include Dan Kimball, Mark Driscoll, and Erwin McManus.

Notes

1. Scot McKnight, "Five Streams of the Emerging Church," *Christianity Today* (online), January 19, 2007, http://www.christianitytoday.com /ct/2007/february/11.35.html.
2. Mark Driscoll, *Confessions of a Reformission Rev* (Grand Rapids: Zondervan, 2006), 22.
3. Tony Jones, *The New Christians: Dispatches from the Emergent Frontier* (San Francisco: Jossey-Bass, 2008), 56.
4. Ibid., xix–xx.
5. Eddie Gibbs and Ryan K. Bolger, *Emerging Churches: Creating Christian Community in Postmodern Cultures* (Grand Rapids: Baker, 2005), 44–45.
6. McKnight, "Five Streams of the Emerging Church."
7. Stanley J. Grenz, A Primer on Postmodernism, Grand Rapids, MI: Wm. B. Eerdmans, 1996, 5, 6
8. The information regarding the brief history of the U. S. movement was adapted from chapter 2 of Jones, *The New Christians*; the Emergent Village website at http://emergentvillage.org/?page_id=42; and two blog posts by Dan Kimball, "Origins of the Terms 'Emerging' and 'Emergent' Church" (parts 1 and 2), http://www.dankimball.com/ vintage_faith/2006/04/origin_of_the_t.html; and http://www. dankimball.com/vintage_faith/2006/04/origins_of_the_.html; accessed January 11, 2012.

Additional Resources

Carson, D. A. *Becoming Conversant with the Emerging Church: Understanding a Movement and Its Implications*. Grand Rapids: Zondervan, 2005.

Henard, William D. and Adam W. Greenway. *Evangelicals Engaging Emergent: A Discussion of the Emergent Church Movement*. Nashville: B&H, 2009.

Gibbs, Eddie, and Ryan K. Bolger. *Emerging Churches: Creating Christian Community in Postmodern Cultures*. Grand Rapids: Baker, 2005.

Jones, Tony. *The New Christians: Dispatches from the Emergent Frontier*. San Francisco: Jossey-Bass, 2008.

Kimball, Dan. *The Emerging Church: Vintage Christianity for New Generations*. Grand Rapids: Zondervan, 2003.

McLaren, Brian D. *A Generous Orthodoxy*. Grand Rapids: Zondervan, 2004.

Pagitt, Doug and Tony Jones, eds. *An Emergent Manifesto of Hope*. Grand Rapids: Baker, 2007.

Sweet, Leonard, ed. *The Church in Emerging Cultures: Five Perspectives*. Grand Rapids: Zondervan, 2003.

Webber, Robert, ed. *Listening to the Beliefs of Emerging Churches: Five Perspectives*. Grand Rapids: Zondervan, 2007.

Yaconelli, Mike, ed. *Stories of Emergence: Moving from Absolute to Authentic*. Grand Rapids: Zondervan, 2003.

6

House Church Movement

There are accounts of house churches (churches meeting in houses) as far back as the New Testament (Acts 2:46; Rom. 16:5; 1 Cor. 16:19; Col. 4:15; Philem. 2), and such meetings continue to this day. In the United States house churches are identified by different names. *Organic* and *simple* are often used as adjectives to distinguish them from more conventional churches. Some will refer to them as "home churches" or the act of being a part of such churches as "home churching" or "house churching."

House churches generally do not view themselves as cells or small groups that are one part of a larger single local church (for cell churches, see chapter 1). Rather, house churches understand themselves to be fully autonomous (each a complete local church) and with their own pastoral leadership (not being overseen by pastors who are physically separate from the group).

Definition

Steve Atkerson has written, " 'House church' is just a convenient label to describe a whole range of topics about the church and how it should function."[1] While the adjective *house* is often used, some churches believe that the word *house* restricts the church to

> ### Church Terminology
>
> Some call them house churches. Some call them organic churches. Some call them simple churches. We prefer to just call them churches. They are rapidly multiplying, simple communities of believers, meeting in homes, offices, campuses, wherever God is moving. This is the pattern common to many parts of the globe, and is now becoming more and more common in the US as well. Where two or more are gathered in His name, there is church. Where "DNA" is present among people, there is church. "D" stands for Divine Truth (loving God/Jesus). "N" stands for Nurturing Relationships (loving one another deeply). "A" stands for Apostolic Mission (being on Jesus' mission to the world). Buildings, programs, and professional clergy are not essential elements of a church. By "simple church," we mean a way of doing and being church that is so simple that any believer would respond by saying, "I could do that!" By "simple church," we mean the kind of church that is described in the New Testament. Not constrained by structure but by the needs of the extended family, and a desire to extend the Kingdom of God. By "simple church," we mean a church that listens to God, follows His leading and obeys His commands. By "simple church," we mean spiritual parents raising spiritual sons and daughters to establish their own families.[2]

a particular meeting place and prefer to use a different term, such as "simple."

Practices

The House Church Movement in the United States is diverse. While many such churches would subscribe to a generally conservative evangelical theology, philosophies and methods of ministry differ from house church to house church. For example, some churches are cessationists, believing that the sign gifts found in the New Testament ceased after the first-century church, while other churches are supportive and regularly encourage the use of such gifts. Some house churches are complementarian, believing that there are different roles for men and women in the churches. Others are egalitarian, believing that all roles and leadership positions are open for anyone, regardless of gender. Some house churches rarely collect an offering, while others do so on a weekly basis.

Some house churches would identify themselves with the larger movement of such churches in the United States simply due to their identity as house churches, but other house churches would not consider themselves attached to any large movement. Beyond size and simplicity, house churches are not the same.

While diversity exists, it is helpful to begin by understanding some of the common characteristics. It is probably best to define these churches not in terms of their sizes or meeting locations but in terms of a "more than, less than" spectrum. In *Missional House Churches: Reaching Our Communities with the Gospel*, I noted that such churches describe themselves in the following ways.[3]

More Organic, Less Institutional. Individuals who are part of house churches rarely refer to the church as a building, location, worship service, or an institutionalized concept, and more in terms of biblical metaphors, like body, bride, fellowship, and community.

More Simple, Less Structure. Such churches attempt to keep all matters of church life as simple as possible, with a fear that complex structures distract from obedience and multiplication. This desire is easily observed in the titles of some house church books: *Simply Church, The Church in the House: A Return to Simplicity*, and *God's Simple Plan for His Church and Your Place in It*.[4]

Characteristics of House Churches

House churches are natural, simple, inexpensive, reproducible, and relational, and have interactive meetings where everyone can participate and use their skills and spiritual gifts to benefit others. This kind of environment strongly fosters discipleship and leadership development. No one falls through the cracks. It is no wonder then that New Testament believers, the early church of the first three centuries, subsequent renewal/reform/revival movements, and the most rapidly growing church planting efforts around the globe today utilize house-sized churches of 10 to 30 people.[5]

More Participatory Worship, Less Passivity. Many house churches operate from the conviction that whenever they gather for worship, everyone is to participate in the gathering (see 1 Cor. 14:26). A high level of accountability is involved, and anonymity is not permitted.

More Community, Less Acquaintances. A great emphasis is placed on genuine community rather than surface-level friendships. Such churches work to create a culture of transparency, accountability, encouragement, confession, and intimacy.

More ministers, Less Ministers. House churches work diligently to remove any barriers between the clergy and laity. Everyone is expected to use his or her gifts and talents to build up the church. The doctrine of the priesthood of the believers is cherished among house churches.

History

House churches in America are not new. It was very common for the early pioneers to gather together to meet in log cabins. However, the contemporary American versions tend to date back to the 1950s with the Charismatic Movement and its ongoing emphasis with the Jesus Movement in the 1960s.[6] While general interest seemed to subside from the 1970s to the 1990s, over the past few years several mainstream media sources have produced stories on house churches. For example, *Dateline* did a television broadcast on house churches on December 9, 2005, and the *700 Club* aired one on January 16, 2006.[7] In addition to numerous stories in local newspapers, major news outlets such as *Time, LA Times, USA Today, Huffington Post*, and the *Denver Post* have also published reports on house churches.[8] Several house church-related books and chapters within books have been published in the past two decades. Interest in U. S. house churches has now garnered international attention;

for example, while writing this book, I was contacted by the largest French Protestant periodical, *Réforme*, for an interview regarding the growth of house churches in the United States.

According to George Barna, the house church has a strong appeal to many Americans: "It is decentralized, has a horizontal structure, exerts low control and authority over its participants, and operates without historical traditions. House churches offer convenience in scheduling and location, are highly relational, and do not waste money on buildings and overhead. They represent the ultimate in flexibility."[9]

This low structure and the high levels of accountability and involvement attract many to participate in these simple expressions of the body of Christ.

Future

Very little research has been conducted on house churches in the United States. George Barna notes that approximately five percent of the American adult population is currently involved with a house church.[10] He expects the numbers of those participating in such churches to grow in the future. Leadership Network did a survey of ninety-seven church planters affiliated with Church Multiplication Associates, a large network of several smaller networks of churches that are typically house churches.[11] According to their findings, thirty percent of the churches studied had started six or more churches. Twenty-two percent had started at least one new church. Eleven percent had started two churches. Eighteen percent had started three churches. Nine percent had started four churches. And another nine percent had started five churches.[12]

While some individuals are attracted to house churches because they have an anti-institutional church attitude or because they are interested in some novel religious experience, there are many house churches working diligently to grow by making disciples and planting new churches.

Recent years has seen the birth and rapid multiplication of house churches in other parts of the world, and has had a direct influence on the propagation of U.S. house churches. The numbers of people coming to faith in Jesus and the number of house churches being birthed have been both rapid and often exponential in growth. Drawing attention to such movements is David Garrison in his book, *Church Planting Movements: How God Is Redeeming a Lost World*.[13] In it he argues that the Lord is reaching the nations with the gospel and simple expressions of local churches are being planted exponentially.

A defining characteristic of the international House Church Movement is that the missionaries planting such churches are keeping their methods simple and helping the churches maintain a simple structure. This low level of complexity assists in the facilitation of rapid multiplication. A growing number of U.S. church planters and churches are attempting to duplicate the movement and keep matters simple for the sake of the health and reproduction of house churches.

In *Missional House Churches*, I examined thirty-three U.S. house churches that had been both baptizing new believers and planting new churches. While these churches were not representative of all of the house churches in the United States, the study did shed some light on an area that is still very much shrouded in darkness. The average size of the churches in this study was between fourteen and sixteen people, although one church was an outlier, having at least thirty-four members. They were located in seventeen states and every region of the country and in both rural and urban contexts. Only one-third of the churches was completely white. Eighty percent had been meeting for fewer than ten years, with five churches at least thirteen years old or older. Each church had baptized at least four to six people in the previous year of the study, and each church had planted between four and six churches in the previous three years.

Notes

1. Steve Atkerson, ed., introduction to *Toward a House Church Theology* (Atlanta: New Testament Restoration Foundation, 1996).
2. http://www.site.house2house.com/about-us/welcome; accessed November 21, 2011.
3. J. D. Payne, *Missional House Churches: Reaching Our Communities with the Gospel* (Colorado Springs: Paternoster, 2008).
4. Tony and Felicity Dale, *Simply Church* (Austin, TX: Karis, 1996); Robert Fitts, *The Church in the House; A Return to Simplicity* (Salem, OR: Preparing the Way Publishers, 2001); and Nate Krupp, *God's Simple Plan for His Church and Your Place in It: A Manual for House Churches*, 2nd ed. (Salem, OR: Preparing the Way Publishers, 1993).
5. Rad Zdero, *Letters to the House Church Movement: Real Letters, Real People, Real Issues* (n.p.: Xulon Press, 2011), 18.
6. C. Kirk Hadaway, Francis M. DuBose, and Stuart A. Wright, *Home Cell Groups and House Churches* (Nashville: Broadman, 1987), 27.
7. For the *Dateline* program see: http://www.youtube.com/watch?v=eubArgoMo-M, uploaded October 24, 2010; accessed November 21, 2011. For one example of some programs on the *700 Club* related to house churches see: http://www.cbn.com/700club/guests/bios/081106tony_felicity_dale.aspx; accessed November 21, 2011.
8. See http://www.time.com/time/magazine/printout/0,8816, 1167737,00.html; http://articles.latimes.com/2007/jul/23/local/me-housechurch23; http://www.usatoday.com/news/religion/2010-07-22-housechurch21_ST_N.htm?loc=interstitialskip; http://www.huffingtonpost.com/2011/04/25/simple-churches-find-a-fo_n_852653.html; and http://www.denverpost.com/frontpage/ci_15547588?source=rss. Accessed November 21, 2011.
9. George Barna, *The Second Coming of the Church* (Nashville: Word, 1998), 180.
10. See Barna Group, "How Many People Really Attend a House Church Barna Study Finds It Depends on the Definition, 2009, http://www.barna.org/barna-update/article/19-organic-church/291-how-many

-people-really-attend-a-house-church-barna-study-finds-it-depends-on
-the-definition; accessed November 21, 2011.

11. Ed Stetzer and Warren Bird, *Viral Churches: Helping Church Planters Become Movement Makers* (San Francisco: Jossey-Bass, 2010), 125. At least two doctoral dissertations have been recently written on house church leadership: Robert Lee Turner, "Leadership Development Process of Select House Church Networks in North America: A Multi-Case Study." The Southern Baptist Theological Seminary, 2011; and John W. Latham, "An Evaluation of Two Selected Contemporary Models of House Church Leadership with an Alternative Proposal." Southeastern Baptist Theological Seminary, 2011.

12. Stetzer and Bird, *Viral Churches*, 125–26.

13. David Garrison, *Church Planting Movements: How God Is Redeeming a Lost World* (Midlothian, VA: WIGTake, 2004).

Additional Resources

Cole, Neil, *Organic Church: Growing Faith Where Life Happens.* San Francisco: Jossey-Bass, 2005.

Dale, Tony and Felicity, *Simply Church.* Austin, TX: Karis Publishing, 2002.

Kreider, Larry. *House Church Networks: A Church for a New Generation.* Ephrata, PA: House to House Publications, 2002.

Payne, J. D. *Missional House Churches: Reaching Our Communities with the Gospel.* Colorado Springs: Paternoster, 2007.

Simpson, Wolfgang. *Houses That Change the World: The Return of the House Churches.* UK: OM Publishing, 1998.

Zdero, Rad. *The Global House Church Movement.* Pasadena, CA: William Carey Library, 2004.

———, ed., *Nexus: The World House Church Movement Reader.* Pasadena, CA: William Carey Library, 2007.

7

Lausanne Movement

The Lausanne Movement is one of the most significant evangelical movements influencing the advancement of the gospel; few movements have had such a global impact. While the origins of the movement can be traced back to the ministry of Billy Graham, the defining date of the movement is July 1974, when the International Congress on Global Evangelization, held in Lausanne, Switzerland (now known as Lausanne I, or simply Lausanne), took place. This event was so significant that John Stott wrote, "'Many a conference has resembled a fireworks display. It has made a loud noise and illuminated the night sky for a few brief brilliant seconds. What is exciting about Lausanne is that its fire continues to spark off other fires.'"[1] What began at Lausanne would carry though the rest of the twentieth century and well into the twenty-first.

Definition

The Lausanne Movement is an international movement that works to mobilize church leaders to partner together for global evangelization.[2] According to the Lausanne Committee for World Evangelization's website, the committee "was to serve as an international catalyst, clearing house, information center, and

Lausanne

Lausanne was a congress that became a movement, an event that became a symbol. As a congress, its purpose was to ask the worldwide church to embrace the task of evangelization in the context of a modern, growing, and increasingly unevangelized world. As a movement, Lausanne had to shape its identity and clearly define its goal: to maintain and expand the momentum for effective world evangelization.[3]

motivational source for evangelization throughout the world. Although not intended to be simply a reaction to the World Council of Churches (WCC), it did serve as an evangelical counterpart to the ecumenical WCC by establishing and fostering an international network of evangelical leaders, as well as periodically sponsoring conferences and consultations."[4]

One can connect with the movement through the Lausanne website (http://www.lausanne.org). In addition to connecting with the movement's leaders according to one's region, people have the option of using the web-based Lausanne Global Conversation site, a free monthly e-newsletter (*Lausanne Connecting Point*), and a free monthly online magazine (*Lausanne World Pulse*).[5]

History

In 1966 the Billy Graham Evangelistic Association and *Christianity Today* cosponsored the World Congress on Evangelism in Berlin. Approximately 1,200 representatives from 100 countries were present during this gathering. Following this event, similar conferences were held in Singapore (1968), Minneapolis (1969), Bogotá (1969), and Australia (1971). Following these events, Billy Graham came to realize that a more diverse congress was needed to "re-frame Christian mission in a world of social, political, economic, and religious upheaval."[6] After discussing his vision with numerous Christian leaders, plans were made for the International Congress on Global Evangelization to be held in Lausanne.

In the summer of 1974, approximately 2,700 Christians representing 151 countries gathered in Lausanne, Switzerland, to address and discuss matters related to global evangelization. Numerous leaders from across the globe gave presentations, later compiled in the book *Let the Earth Hear His Voice*.

Over the next fifteen years, several Lausanne-related conferences took place in various locations across the world. However, it was not until July 1989 in Manila, Philippines, that the second major world congress occurred (Lausanne II). The presentations of this congress were published in the book *Proclaim Christ Until He Comes: Calling the Whole Church to Take the Whole Gospel to the Whole World*.

Gatherings related to the Lausanne Movement have often resulted in the production of documents known as Lausanne Occasional Papers. These periodic publications are the result of numerous committee members working together to address theological and cultural issues affecting the advancement of the gospel. At the time of this writing, sixty-five such papers are available. Some of the topics include witnessing to Muslims/Hindus/Animists/nominal Christians, marketplace ministry, ministry among people with disabilities, redeeming the arts, prayer and evangelism, evangelizing children, diasporas, theological education, and business as mission.

The third global congress took place in Cape Town, South Africa, on October 16–25, 2010. Lausanne III gathered 4,000 delegates from 198 countries. The purpose of the event "was to re-stimulate the spirit of Lausanne, as represented in The Lausanne Covenant, and so to promote unity, humility in service, and a call to active global evangelization."[7] For the first time in the movement's history, sessions were put online and were broadcast to thousands around the world to 650 designated viewing sites in 91 countries. A specific network of Cape Town 2010 bloggers was established as well as a website for anyone to dialogue about the issues leading up to and during the meeting.

In addition to Lausanne III being the first conference in the movement's history to be "wired" to the global community, it was also the first such gathering to limit the number of representatives and speakers from Western countries. This ensured that the proportion of Western Christians to majority world Christians at the gathering would be more representative of the worldwide church. In addition to reaffirming numerous biblical truths about missions, the congress also addressed many of the contemporary challenges facing gospel advancement in the twenty-first century.

A confession of faith and call to action known as the Cape Town Commitment was drafted for the event. In addition to this document, the Cape Town 2010 Advance Papers and other relevant articles were produced.[8]

Important Contributions

Numerous contributions have been made to the advancement of the gospel over the nearly four decades of the movement. Some of these have been changes made by individual Christians in their belief and practice; others have been on a macro level resulting in shifts across denominations and mission agencies.

While the movement continues to advance, three congresses and decades of time allow for some comment regarding the significant aspects of the movement. The following are some of the emphases and outcomes of the congresses that have influenced evangelical thought.

The Covenant. The Lausanne Covenant was introduced in Lausanne I and quickly became the most influential document produced by evangelicals to guide partnerships and missionary labors in the twentieth century. The drafting committee of the covenant was chaired by John Stott, who has also been called the chief architect of the document. The covenant addresses the following fifteen categories affecting evangelical theology and cooperation among evangelicals for global evangelization:

- The Purpose of God

- The Authority and Power of the Bible

- The Uniqueness and Universality of Christ

- The Nature of Evangelism

- Christian Social Responsibility

- The Church and Evangelism

- Cooperation in Evangelism

- Churches in Evangelistic Partnership

- The Urgency of the Evangelistic Task

- Evangelism and Culture

- Education and Leadership

- Spiritual Conflict

- Freedom and Persecution

- The Power of the Holy Spirit

- The Return of Christ

Relationship Between Evangelism and Social Responsibility. Debates regarding the mission of the church took place in the mid-twentieth century among evangelicals. Is evangelism the primary work of the church, or is social ministry (meeting the physical, emotional, and social needs of others)? Or is it both? Is the church to preach the good news of Jesus, calling people to repentance and faith, or to reform society? Is the priority on proclamation or giving a cup of water to those in need?

The Lausanne Covenant addressed this issue. While giving priority to evangelism, it advocated that the church has a social responsibility as well. In Article 6 on "The Church and Evangelism," the covenant states: "In the Church's mission of sacrificial service evangelism is primary." This statement, however, follows Article 5 "Christian Social Responsibility," which points to the fact that the church is to love neighbor as self:

> We affirm that God is both the Creator and the Judge of all people. We therefore should share his concern for justice and reconciliation throughout human society and for the liberation of men and women from every kind of oppression. Because men and women are made in the image of God, every person, regardless of race, religion, colour, culture, class, sex or age, has an intrinsic dignity because of which he or she should be respected and served, not exploited. Here too we express penitence both for our neglect and for having sometimes regarded evangelism and social concern as mutually exclusive. Although reconciliation with other people is not reconciliation with God, nor is social action evangelism, nor is political liberation salvation, nevertheless we affirm that evangelism and socio-political involvement are both part of our Christian duty. For both are necessary expressions of our doctrines of God and man, our love for our neighbour and our obedience to Jesus Christ. The message of salvation implies also a message of judgment upon every form of alienation, oppression and discrimination, and we should not be afraid to denounce evil and injustice wherever they exist. When people receive Christ they are born again into his kingdom and must seek not only to exhibit but also to spread its righteousness in the midst of an unrighteous world. The salvation

we claim should be transforming us in the totality of our personal and social responsibilities. Faith without works is dead.[9]

A minority group attending Lausanne I and the Lausanne Consultation in Pattaya, Thailand, in 1980 "strongly objected to prioritizing the evangelistic mandate,"[10] according to C. Peter Wagner. As a result of their concern, another consultation was held in 1982 in Grand Rapids, Michigan, to discuss the relationship between evangelism and social responsibility. The Lausanne Occasional Paper No. 22, in which a statement reaffirming the priority of evangelism was made, was published:

Seldom if ever should we have to choose between satisfying physical hunger and spiritual hunger, or between healing bodies and saving souls, since an authentic love for our neighbour will lead us to serve him or her as a whole person. Nevertheless, if we must choose, then we have to say that the supreme and ultimate need of all humankind is the saving grace of Jesus Christ, and that therefore a person's eternal, spiritual salvation is of greater importance than his or her temporal and material well-being (cf. 2 Cor. 4:16–18).[11]

In 2004, a forum was hosted in Pattaya, Thailand, where the discussion of this relationship continued and the Lausanne Occasional Paper No. 33, "Holistic Mission," was published.[12] In this document the authors were not in favor of giving priority to evangelism. While the original covenant remains the tether to which those within the movement hold fast, there does appear to be a growing number of evangelicals who are not content with the 1974 expression of the relationship of evangelism and social responsibility.

Unreached People Groups. Possibly the most influential contribution of the movement, with the exception of the Covenant, has been the emphasis on evangelizing the world's unreached people groups. Ralph D. Winter delivered an address to the Congress of

Lausanne I, titled "The Highest Priority: Cross-Cultural Evangelism," in which he argued that the majority of the unbelievers in the world will only hear the gospel if missionaries cross significant cultural barriers in order to reach them. He lamented, "Most non-Christians in the world today are not culturally near neighbors of any Christians."[13] He argued that a radically different approach to doing evangelism is required when making such cultural leaps. Until every people group has a thriving church within it that can carry out the work of evangelism, it will continue to be necessary for missionaries to cross large cultural gaps in order to evangelize.

Winter went on to show that most Christians do not know how many people groups exist in the world without a thriving church. This "people blindness" stemmed from Christians failing to understand the nations of the world as differing people groups but rather viewing the nation as geopolitical locations. For example, as long as there was a church in Indonesia, many Christians thought the gospel had reached the entire nation. Winter argued that the nation of Indonesia contains numerous cultures, many without a thriving church, and most people in Indonesia will only be able to hear and understand the gospel if someone from a vastly different culture—even another Indonesian culture—crosses the cultural barriers to share the message. It was this address that raised the banner for the urgent need to understand the people groups of the world and the necessity for cross-cultural evangelism that results in new churches.

Development of Partnerships. Lausanne II was comprised of 3,000 participants from 170 countries. The resulting document of this gathering was the Manila Manifesto, a declaration of thirty-one clauses that further elaborated on the Lausanne Covenant of 1974. This gathering also served as a catalyst for the development of more than three hundred partnerships and new initiatives.[14]

Significance of the Majority World Church. While Lausanne II gave attention to the growth of the church across the majority world, Lausanne III, held in Cape Town, South Africa, attempted to provide a fair representation of participants from the majority world. The church was growing faster and has more members from the non-Western world than from the West. Because Lausanne III was held in 2010, it is still too early to determine the outcome of the attention given to the majority world. However, Lausanne III has helped the church in the West recognize the importance of the majority world church, which is now being seen as an equal partner in the global advancement of the gospel.

Leaders

Some of the most influential evangelical Christian leaders have been involved with the movement since 1974. Once the names of the various committee members are included, the list contains almost all of the most influential evangelicals from across the world. While space does not permit the listing of those names, this chapter does demand the mention of the two most significant, without whom the movement would not have started. The labors of Billy Graham and John Stott were instrumental in gathering such global leaders together in 1974, 1989, and 2010, and served to stimulate the movement's momentum.

There are no official headquarters for the Lausanne Movement; names of individuals who provide executive, regional, advisory, and issue-based leadership to the movement are found on the Lausanne website.[15]

Notes

1. http://www.lausanne.org/en/about; accessed December 28, 2011.
2. http://www.lausanne.org/en/about/faqs.html; accessed May 29, 2012.

3. Valdir R. Steuernagel, "Social Concern and Evangelization: The Journey of the Lausanne Movement," *International Bulletin of Missionary Research* 15, no. 2 (April 1991), 53.
4. http://www.lausanne.org/en/gatherings/lausanne-1974/historical -background.html; accessed October 27, 2011.
5. http://www.lausanne.org/en/about.html.
6. Ibid.
7. Ibid.
8. For access to these resources, see http://www.lausanne.org/en /documents/cape-town-2010.html; accessed December 28, 2011.
9. http://www.lausanne.org/en/documents/lausanne-covenant.html; accessed December 28, 2011.
10. C. Peter Wagner, *Strategies for Church Growth: Tools for Effective Mission and Evangelism* (Ventura, CA: Regal, 1989), 106.
11. "Evangelism and Social Responsibility: An Evangelical Commitment," Lausanne Occasional Paper 21, http://www.lausanne.org/en /documents/lops/79-lop-21.html; accessed December 28, 2011.
12. http://www.lausanne.org/docs/2004forum/LOP33_IG4.pdf; accessed December 28, 2011.
13. Ralph D. Winter, "The Highest Priority: Cross-Cultural Evangelism," in J. D. Douglas, ed., *Let the Earth Hear His Voice: International Congress on World Evangelization, Lausanne, Switzerland* (Minneapolis: World Wide Publications, 1975), 213.
14. http://www.lausanne.org/en/about.html.
15. http://www.lausanne.org/en/about/leadership.html; accessed October 27, 2011.

Additional Resources

Douglas, J. D., ed. *Let the Earth Hear His Voice: International Congress on World Evangelization, Lausanne, Switzerland*. Minneapolis: World Wide Publications, 1975.

———*Proclaim Christ Until He Comes: Calling the Whole Church to Take the Whole Gospel to the Whole World*. Minneapolis: World Wide Publications, 1990.

The Lausanne Covenant is available at http://www.lausanne.org/en/documents /lausanne-covenant.html.

The Manila Manifesto is available at http://www.lausanne.org/en/documents /manila-manifesto.html.

The Cape Town Commitment is available at http://www.lausanne.org/docs/CapeTownCommitment.pdf.

Lausanne Occasional Papers are available at http://www.lausanne.org/en/documents/lops.html.

8

Megachurch Movement

Megachurches are not unique to the United States; in fact, the largest churches in the world exist outside of North America.[1] The influence of such churches is felt across the United States. Megachurches often develop programs and resources that are influential among other churches. Their leaders are many times consulted by leaders in other churches. While the number of megachurches in the United States only comprise 0.3 percent of all of the country's churches, they involve almost 10 percent of the nation's weekly Protestant worshippers.[2]

Definition

The most common way to define a megachurch is by the number of weekly attendants. A megachurch is a church that has at least two thousand people present for its weekend worship gatherings. In other ways, the churches can be quite disparate. Such churches can differ significantly when it comes to theological convictions, worship styles, leadership, and organizational structures. While many megachurches consider themselves to be nondenominational (34 percent), they are also found within mainstream denominations, including Baptists, Assemblies of God, United Methodists,

Lutherans (ELCA), Presbyterians (PCUSA), Disciples of Christ, Church of Christ, Calvary Chapel, Four Square, and Vineyard.[3]

History

The megachurch is as old as the first church in Jerusalem—Luke wrote that the membership of the church in that city was several thousand in number—but as a contemporary movement related to the United States, the rise of megachurches began in the nineteenth century.[4] At the beginning of the twentieth century, six such churches existed, with the number increasing to sixteen in 1960.[5] It was during the latter half of the twentieth century that the proliferation of megachurches occurred, with the Hartford Institute for Religion Research estimating that there are more than twelve hundred megachurches in the United States.[6] Transportation and other societal shifts are seen as contributing factors to such growth. For example, from a sociological perspective, as the automobile became a common item in the lives of most Americans, they became more mobile and able to reach locations in less time and with greater ease. Americans became more comfortable with large shopping districts, and began to expect a high degree of professionalism and quality. No longer were Americans confined to a particular parish. They now had choices even related to their churches, and the ability to commute to Sunday gatherings.

Some of the best and most extensive research on megachurches in the United States has been conducted by the Hartford Institute for Religion Research (Scott Thumma) and Leadership Network (Dave Travis and Warren Bird). Both of these organizations have invested substantial time and resources into better understanding the world of the megachurch. According to Thumma and Travis, the estimated number of megachurches in the United States is increasing by about fifty churches each year.[7]

Characteristics

In 2005, Thumma, Travis, and Bird released a summary report of the research findings of the efforts by Hartford Seminary, Hartford Institute for Religion Research, and Leadership Network. This report offered a glimpse of the characteristics of megachurches in the United States.[8]

- The typical megachurch ranges in size from two thousand to three thousand people.
- Only 16 percent of megachurches have five thousand or more people in weekly attendance.
- The states with the greatest concentrations of megachurches are California (14 percent), Texas (13 percent), Florida (7 percent), and Georgia (6 percent).
- 15 percent of megachurches have been started in the past fifteen years.
- 35 to 40 percent of megachurches are nondenominational.
- The denominations with the largest numbers of megachurches in the study were Southern Baptist (20 percent), United Methodist (9 percent), and Assemblies of God (5 percent).
- The majority of such churches identified themselves as Evangelical (56 percent), Pentecostal (8 percent), or Charismatic (8 percent).
- The churches averaged twenty full-time paid leadership staff positions and nine part-time administrative or support staff positions.
- 58 percent indicated that evangelism was a key activity of the church.

A portion of the report was developed to address some widely held assumptions regarding megachurches. According to the researchers, the following are eleven myths and facts about such churches.

Myth: All megachurches are alike.
Fact: Differences exist regarding growth rates, sizes, and emphases.

Myth: All megachurches are equally good at being big.
Fact: While some understand how to function as a large institution, others struggle and even decline.

Myth: There is an over-emphasis of money in all the megachurches.
Fact: Money is a low priority, except during a building or capital campaign.

Myth: Megachurches are just spectator worship and are not serious about Christianity.
Fact: Most megachurches have high expectations and are serious about orthodox beliefs and preaching.

Myth: These churches only care about themselves.
Fact: Considerable outreach and social ministry is taking place among megachurches on local, regional, and global scales.

Myth: All megachurches are major political players and pawns or powerbrokers to the Republican Party.
Fact: While a few megachurches are vocally politically active, a majority of megachurches surveyed stated they are not politically active.

Myth: All megachurches have huge sanctuaries and enormous campuses.

Fact: "Mega" refers to attendance, not building size. Many churches have multiple worship gatherings and even use multiple locations for church gatherings.

Myth: All megachurches are nondenominational.

Fact: The majority of megachurches belong to some denomination.

Myth: All megachurches are homogeneous congregations with little diversity.

Fact: A large and growing number of such churches are intentionally multiethnic.

Myth: Megachurches grow primarily because of great programming.

Fact: Megachurches grow because of the invitations extended by attendees to people they know.

Myth: The megachurch phenomenon is over and on the decline. Younger generations are not interested in such churches.

Fact: The number of megachurches continue to grow, with many made up of people under thirty-five years of age.

Leaders

The Leadership Network conducted a survey of 232 megachurch pastors in 2009. While pastors from thirty-eight states were represented, a few were from other countries—including four from Canada. The following are some of the noteworthy findings related to these leaders.[9]

- The average age for a megachurch pastor is fifty-one years.

- The typical responder was white, married for twenty-seven years, had two children living at home, and voted Republican.

- When asked to select from nine possible options, 81 percent viewed their role as "preacher-teacher" as compared to 16 percent who viewed their role as "pastor."

- 77 percent chose leadership as one of their top three spiritual gifts, followed by teaching at 67 percent.

- 1 percent considered the visitation of members, sick, and shut-ins as an area of strength.

- The typical senior pastor has been on staff at the current church for sixteen years.

- 74 percent of the senior pastors have a master's degree or doctorate in theology.

- When compared to other pastors, megachurch pastors:

  - Are less likely to be single, divorced, or re-married

  - Are more likely to have a doctoral degree

  - Are just as likely to report satisfaction with their salary/benefits/housing/living arrangements

  - Are less satisfied with their spiritual life and leadership effectiveness

  - Take more time off each week

  - Experience less conflict in the churches

- ○ Are more likely to receive an annual performance review

- ○ Report higher levels of congregational morale

- ○ Lead churches that are open to trying new things

Congregation

In a study of almost twenty-five thousand responses from twelve carefully selected U.S. megachurches, Thumma and Bird have provided the following findings relating to those who attend such churches. Surprisingly, the megachurch attendee is very similar to the average attendee of smaller congregations. In general the typical profile is female, highly educated, middle class, married, and has children. However, upon closer examination, significant differences emerge among the congregations of megachurches, where there is a larger percentage of younger adults/singles, a higher concentration of wealth, and more education.[10]

Findings:

- Almost 75 percent of megachurch attendees come from other churches (some nearby and some distant), a figure that is only 6 percent higher than congregations of all sizes.

- The average megachurch attendee is forty years of age.

- Approximately a third of megachurch attendees are single compared to 10 percent in the typical congregation.

- 60 percent of attendees are involved in small groups.

- 45 percent of attendees believed their spiritual needs are being met, compared to 38 percent of the responders from churches of all sizes.

- 82 percent of attendees came as a result of the invitation of a friend, family member, or coworker.

Churches

According to *Outreach Magazine*, the following were the largest churches in the United States in 2010.[11]

- Lakewood Church, Houston, Texas: average attendance of 43,500.

- North Point Community Church, Alpharetta, Georgia: average attendance of 24,325.

- Second Baptist Church, Houston, Texas: average attendance of 24,041.

- Willow Creek Community Church, South Barrington, Illinois: average attendance of 24,000.

- Southeast Christian Church, Louisville, Kentucky: average attendance of 19,230.

- Saddleback Church, Lake Forest, California: average attendance of 18,763.

- Woodlands Church, The Woodlands, Texas: average attendance of 18,322.

- Phoenix First Assembly of God, Phoenix, Arizona: average attendance of 16,660.

- Central Christian Church, Henderson, Nevada: average attendance of 16,582.

- Calvary Chapel Fort Lauderdale, Fort Lauderdale, Florida: average attendance of 15,560.

Notes

1. For an extensive list of many of the world's megachurches, see http://innovationlab.leadnet.org/warren/?/world/; accessed November 11, 2011.
2. Warren Bird, "Teacher First: Leadership Network's 2009 Large-Church Senior Pastor Survey," July 14, 2009, http://leadnet.org/resources/download/teacher_first_2009_survey_large_church_senior_pastors; downloaded November 11, 2011; http://www.religiontoday.com/blog/some-fear-megachurch-bubble-may-soon-burst.html; accessed June 26, 2012.
3. Scott Thumma and Dave Travis, *Beyond Megachurch Myths: What We Can Learn from America's Largest Churches* (San Francisco: Jossey-Bass, 2007), 27.
4. Ibid., 24.
5. Scott Thumma, Dave Travis, and Warren Bird, "Megachurches Today 2005: Summary of Research Findings," 1, http://hirr.hartsem.edu/megachurch/megastoday2005summaryreport.pdf; accessed November 11, 2011.
6. http://hirr.hartsem.edu/megachurch/definition.html; accessed November 11, 2011.
7. Thumma and Travis, *Beyond Megachurch Myths*, 6.
8. Thumma, Travis, and Bird, "Megachurches Today 2005."
9. Bird, "Teacher First."
10. Scott Thumma and Warren Bird, "Not Who You Think They Are," June 2009, http://hirr.hartsem.edu/megachurch/National%20Survey%20of%20Megachurch%20Attenders%20-final.pdf; accessed November 17, 2011.
11. "Outreach Largest and Fastest Growing Churches in America," annual issue *Outreach Magazine*, September 15, 2010, 35.

Additional Resources

Guinness, Os. *Dining with the Devil: The Megachurch Movement Flirts with Modernity*. Grand Rapids: Baker, 1993.

Hybels, Lynne and Bill. *Rediscovering Church: The Story and Vision of Willow Creek Community Church*. Grand Rapids, MI: Zondervan Publishing House, 1995.

Outreach Magazine. An annual report is included on the top one hundred largest and one hundred fastest-growing churches in the United States.

Russell, Bob. *When God Builds a Church: 10 Principles for Growing a Dynamic Church*. New York: Howard, 2000.

Thumma, Scott and Dave Travis, *Beyond Megachurch Myths: What We Can Learn from America's Largest Churches*. San Francisco: Jossey-Bass, 2007.

Warren, Rick. *The Purpose Driven Church: Growth Without Compromising Your Message and Mission*. Grand Rapids: Zondervan, 1995. While not a book on megachurches, Warren does share the story and missiological principles of how his church became a megachurch.

9

Missional Church Movement

The end of the twentieth century saw the birth of the Missional Church Movement, a movement that would dominate many evangelical discussions in the United States in the decade following. Beginning in Europe and significantly shaped by mainline leadership in the United States, evangelicals were critical and slow to embrace this new paradigm. However, once they welcomed this contemporary thinking regarding ecclesiological issues, they began to champion the cause.

Definition

Missional is an adjective that derives from an understanding of God as a missionary God who has redeemed the church and called them to join in the mission (*missio Dei*) of making disciples among the nations of the world. A missional church is one that maintains an outward focus. A missional church does not have missions as simply a program or an event, but rather, a missional church exists for the mission of God. Missional churches understand their contexts and function to be missionaries wherever they are located. A missional church submits to God's mission and follows the Spirit's leadership in Jesus' plan for building his church.

The word *missional* was first used in the 1883 book *The Heroes of African Discovery and Adventure, from the Death of Livingstone to the Year 1882* and referred to a bishop of Central Africa. The word was then used in several contexts across the twentieth century, culminating in its widespread popularity at the turn of the century.[1]

Since the seminal publication *Missional Church: A Vision for the Sending of the Church in North America* by Darrell L. Guder, several books related to the "missional" idea and networks embracing this paradigm have developed. Churches and denominations now use the word *missional* in their documents; each year, conferences and seminars are offered on the topic; and schools have embraced the word in their literature and degree programs. From the academy to the marketplace, the word *missional* is widely used.

History

A renewed sense of the missionary nature of the church arose in the 1930s through the works of Karl Barth and Karl Hartenstein.[2] Theologians began to argue for a "theocentric" (God-centered) approach rather than an "ecclesiolocentric" (church-centered) approach to missionary work. For years, Christian missions was closely tied to the cultural expressions of the European—and eventually, North American—church. Mission was understood as a work of the church that involved introducing unbelieving nations both to Jesus and to Western civilization. Christendom had run its course, but the church was still attempting to operate as if nothing had shifted.

Theologians began to argue that the focus should be on the *missio Dei* (mission of God) rather than on the mission of the church. Conversations regarding ecclesiology, *missio Dei*, and the kingdom of God within the International Missionary Council and the World Council of Churches, Vatican II, and multiple midcentury church mergers in the United States contributed to what has become known as the missional church.[3] According to Craig Van Gelder and Dwight J. Zscheile, "With this shift in perspective, the primary agency for mission moves to divine initiative through the ministry of the Spirit as the larger framework within which our human responses take place."[4] Under this paradigm, the church recognizes that God is currently at work in the world and understands itself as joining God in this mission.

While several gatherings of the International Missionary Council and the World Council of Churches over the course of the mid-twentieth century helped shape the theological underpinnings of what would become the Missional Church Movement, it was the writings of Lesslie Newbigin that connected with many in the United Kingdom in the 1980s. Newbigin returned to the West after serving for decades as a missionary in India and found that the church had fallen from the place of cultural prominence it had when he first set off for South Asia.

Newbigin's small 1983 monograph published by the World Council of Churches, *The Other Side of 1984: Questions for the Churches*, raised significant questions regarding what a renewed missionary encounter with Western civilization should look like. Western society had separated faith from facts, relegating the former to the private sphere of life and the latter to the public domain. Newbigin saw that the church was no longer society's center of authority and counsel. He wrote:

> What I am pleading for is a genuinely missionary encounter with post-Enlightenment culture. We have too long accepted the position of a privileged option for the private sector. We have been tempted either to withdraw into an intellectual ghetto, seeking to preserve a kind of piety in church and home while leaving the public world (including the world of scholarship) to be governed by another ideology. Or we have been tempted to regard the "modern

scientific world-view" as though it were simply a transcript of reality which we must—willy-nilly—accept as true. We then try to adjust our Christian beliefs to the requirements of "modern thought" and to find some room for ideas, sentiments and policies which are suggested to us by the Christian tradition—but always within the framework of the "modern scientific world-view." A truly missionary approach would reject both of these strategies; would recognize frankly the fact that the Christian dogma offers a "fiduciary framework" quite different from and (in some respects) incompatible with the framework within which modern European culture has developed; and would be quite bold and uncompromising in setting forth the Christian "dogma", but also very humble and teachable in engaging in dialogue with those who live by other fundamental beliefs.[5]

This "genuinely missionary encounter" would become the missiological force behind the Missional Church Movement. Conversations began to spill over into North America, and by the late 1980s the Gospel and Our Culture Network emerged. This network began to apply Newbigin's thoughts and began to wrestle with the details of this desired "encounter." Its purpose was threefold:

1. To discern how the church in North America is called anew to receive and participate in the mission of the triune God, within a variety of cultural and social settings.
2. To clarify the nature of the interaction between gospel, culture, and church, which both shapes that mission and is shaped by it.
3. To discover models of the church in North America capable of sustaining an effective and faithful witness to the gospel, appropriate to various and current emerging contexts.[6]

It was in 1998 that Darrell L. Guder edited the book *Missional Church: A Vision for the Sending of the Church in North America* as a response to Newbigin's missionary call. Guder worked with an ecumenical team of six missiologists to produce this seminal work, in which the authors attempt to establish a theological foundation for the church that understands that North America is a mission field and the church needs to respond properly. This book was the beginning of several related and influential publications of the Gospel and Our Culture Network addressing the need to shift from an ecclesiocentric mission to a theocentric mission:

> This ecclesiocentric understanding of mission has been replaced during this century by a profoundly theocentric reconceptualization of Christian mission. We have come to see that mission is not merely an activity of the church. Rather, mission is the result of God's initiative, rooted in God's purposes to restore and heal creation. "mission" means "sending," and it is the central biblical theme describing the purpose of God's action in human history. God's mission began with the call of Israel to receive God's blessings in order to be a blessing to the nations. God's mission unfolded in the history of God's people across the centuries recorded in Scripture, and it reached its revelatory climax in the incarnation of God's work of salvation in Jesus' ministering, crucified, and resurrected. God's mission continued then in the sending of the Spirit to call forth and empower the church as the witness to God's good news in Jesus Christ. It continues today in the worldwide witness of churches in every culture to the gospel of Jesus Christ, and it moves toward the promised consummation of God's salvation in the *eschaton* ("last" or "final day").[7]

Under this new mission of God (*missio Dei*) paradigm the church is understood as a people devoted to the mission of God. Mission is not reduced to one program among several church activities but is the main activity of the church. According to Guder,

"Our challenge today is to move from church with mission to missional church."[8]

Practices

While the movement is not very old, it has already fragmented, with movements in differing directions. These movements that have branched off have resulted in a great deal of complexity, with each branch having its own advocates. Craig Van Gelder and Dwight J. Zscheile separate these movements into four categories:[9]

> The dividing line between branches revolves around the extent to which one starts with the *mission of the church* and the extent to which one starts with the *mission of God;* when starting with the mission of God, it also has to do with how robust the Trinitarian theology is.... The key question is: how do we understand God's presence in the world, in general, and in the midst of the church, in particular?[10]

Discovering. Advocates in this category are beginning to consider the missional conversation. They tend to refer to mission in more traditional language and to focus on some combination of the following: (1) obedience to the Great Commission and Great Commandment; (2) christiology as the beginning point for mission; (3) the dichotomy of incarnational ministry (an approach whereby church members seek to live their lives among unbelievers so that through their words and actions they may be able to reach them with the gospel) and attractional ministry (an approach whereby a church seeks to create an evangelistic event whereby church members are able to invite unbelievers to attend, participate, and hear the gospel); and (4) the church as the location of God's work today.

Utilizing. Leaders in this category draw from the original ideas in *Missional Church*. They work to understand the implications of these ideas on the church and tend to emphasize some combination of the following: (1) the church is called to participate in the mission of God; (2) understanding God's reign is important to understanding his global mission; and (3) the church is required to engage with the world (with different definitions of "engage" being represented).

Engaging. Leaders found within this category have accepted and assume the biblical and theological ideas associated with the Missional Church Movement, including the theocentric approach to the mission of God in the world. Much of their writings focus on the practical application and implications of the missional conversation.

Extending. Those who reside in this category have not only embraced the original thoughts of the missional conversation but are laboring to expand and develop the initial arguments. Much of their work involves developing the biblical and theological frameworks that define the parameters for the conversation.

Beliefs

Since there are many proponents of the movement and no one central organizational headquarters, it is difficult to articulate the common convictions of the movement today. However, the writings of those who have been involved in the movement's early days is helpful.

According to Craig Van Gelder, missional churches must have a self-awareness of the missionary nature of the church:

> The genetic code of missional church means it is missionary in its very essence. This means that congregations exist in the world as being missionary in nature. The self-understanding of such

congregations is not first of all being established (that they represent the primary location of God's activity in the world), or being corporate (that they do something on behalf of God in the world), but rather their self-understanding is missional (they participate through the Spirit's leading in what God is doing in the world).[11]

In addition to this self-understanding, six common convictions are found in the movement.

1. The church in North America is now located within a dramatically changed context.
2. The good news of the gospel announced by Jesus needs to shape the identity of the missional church.
3. The missional church, with its identity rooted in the reign of God, must live as an alternative community in the world.
4. The missional church needs to understand that the Holy Spirit cultivates communities that represent the reign of God.
5. The missional leadership focuses on equipping all of God's people for mission.
6. The missional church needs to develop structures for shaping its life and ministry as well as to practice connectedness within the larger church.[12]

Some individuals have attempted to delineate the specific practical implications of missional thought on local churches. Milfred Minatrea, for example, noted that such churches have the following practices:

- They have a high threshold for membership (clear membership expectations).

- They are real, not real religious (relationships among members are not superficial).

- They teach to obey, rather than to know (faith has practical implications).

- They rewrite worship every week (worship is about content not form).

- They live apostolically (members are sent into the world to be on mission).

- They expect to change the world (relationships are the key to global transformation).

- They order actions according to purpose (specific reasons guide the labors).

- They measure growth by capacity to release, not retain (equipping and sending is the norm).

- They place kingdom concerns first (kingdom issues take priority over denominational issues).[13]

Leaders

Numerous leaders have contributed to the movement over the past eighty years; readers will find the works of the following people an excellent place to begin reading about the movement and its developments. Early to mid-twentieth-century theologians, including Karl Barth, Karl Hartenstein, Oscar Cullman, Johannes Blauw, and Johannes Hoekendijk influenced the birth of the movement. Missiologists and missionaries such as Hendrik Kraemer, Lesslie Newbigin, and David Bosch added to the development of thought behind what would eventually become the movement. Within

North America, the original contributors to *Missional Church* provided the momentum behind the movement and assisted in its maturation: Darrell L. Guder, Lois Barrett, Inagrace T. Dietterich, George R. Hunsberger, Alan J. Roxburgh, and Craig Van Gelder. Other significant missiologists and popular authors include: Francis Dubose, Wilbert Shenk, Charles Van Engen, Ed Stetzer, Michael Frost, Alan Hirsch, M. Scott Boren, Milfred Minatrea, and Reggie McNeal.

Notes

1. Craig Van Gelder and Dwight J. Zscheile, *The Missional Church in Perspective: Mapping Trends and Shaping the Conversation* (Grand Rapids: Baker, 2011), 42–47.
2. Tiina Ahonen, "Antedating Missional Church: David Bosch's Views on the Missionary Nature of the Church and on the Missionary Structure of the Congregation," *Swedish Missiological Themes* 92, no. 4 (2004): 576.
3. Craig Van Gelder, "From Corporate Church to Missional Church: The Challenge Facing Congregations Today," *Review and Expositor* 101 (Summer 2004): 427.
4. Van Gelder and Zscheile, *The Missional Church in Perspective*, 8.
5. Lesslie Newbigin, *The Other Side of 1984: Questions for the Churches* (Geneva: World Council of Churches, 1983), 31–32.
6. John R. "Pete" Hendrick, "Congregations with Missions vs. Missionary Congregations," in George R. Hunsberger and Craig Van Gelder, eds., *Church Between Gospel and Culture: The Emerging Mission in North America* (Grand Rapids: Eerdmans), 303.
7. Darrell L. Guder, ed., *Missional Church: A Vision for the Sending of the Church in North America* (Grand Rapids: Eerdmans, 1998), 4.
8. Ibid., 6.
9. Van Gelder and Zscheile, *The Missional Church in Perspective*, 67–98.
10. Ibid., 69.
11. Craig Van Gelder, "From Corporate Church to Missional Church": 446.
12. Van Gelder and Zscheile, *The Missional Church in Perspective*, 49, 50, 51.
13. Milfred Minatrea, *Shaped by God's Heart: The Passion and Practices of Missional Churches* (San Francisco: Jossey-Bass, 2004).

Additional Resources

Bosch, David J. *Transforming Mission: Paradigm Shifts in Theology of Mission.* Maryknoll, NY: Orbis Books, 1991.

Frost, Michael, and Alan Hirsch, *The Shaping of Things to Come: Innovation and Mission for the 21st Century Church.* Peabody, MA: Hendrickson, 2003.

Guder, Darrell L., ed., *Missional Church: A Vision for the Sending of the Church in North America.* Grand Rapids: Eerdmans, 1998.

Hunsberger, George R., and Craig Van Gelder, eds. *Church Between Gospel and Culture: The Emerging Mission in North America.* Grand Rapids: Eerdmans, 1996.

Minatrea, Milfred. *Shaped by God's Heart: The Passion and Practices of Missional Churches.* San Francisco: Jossey-Bass, 2004.

Newbigin, Lesslie. *Foolishness to the Greeks: The Gospel and Western Culture.* Grand Rapids: Eerdmans, 1986.

———. *The Other Side of 1984: Questions for the Churches.* Geneva: World Council of Churches, 1983.

Van Gelder, Craig, and Dwight J. Zscheile. *The Missional Church in Perspective: Mapping Trends and Shaping the Conversation.* Grand Rapids: Baker, 2011.

10

Multisite Church Movement

The Multisite Church Movement developed quickly in the first decade of the twenty-first century. While churches that meet in more than one location or site have been around for decades, their numbers have dramatically increased in recent years. The growth and interest in the multisite paradigm developed such momentum that in 2006, Geoff Surratt, Greg Ligon, and Warren Bird predicted that thirty thousand American churches "will be multi-site within the next few years."[1] The movement has garnered the attention of the secular media, with news outlets such as the *Chicago Tribune* and National Public Radio producing stories on the multisite church.[2]

While having multiple campuses frees up space and can be part of a growth strategy, Bill Easum and Dave Travis advocate that "mission, rather than space, determines the agenda." According to them, the key to understanding the movement is to recognize that the Great Commission is the driving factor behind the movement.[3]

Definition

A multisite congregation defines itself in terms of the number of locations for weekly worship gatherings. Although this is similar to the Cell Church Movement, the difference is that a cell church would be comprised of many cells (small groups) that would gather corporately each week for worship. A multisite church would have large groups gathering for corporate worship in different locations, with those groups (campuses) oftentimes consisting of their own small groups (cells). A multisite church would not think of its campuses as cells. At present, there are two definitions regarding what constitutes a multisite church, one restrictive and the other more inclusive. The restrictive definition limits multisite church to one that has started another site in a location other than their present campus.[4] The general definition is more inclusive, including meetings both on- and off-site. As an example of the latter: "A multisite church is one church meeting in multiple locations—different rooms on the same campus, different locations in the same region, or in some instances, different cities, states, or nations. A multi-site church shares a common vision, budget, leadership, and board."[5]

According to Surratt, Ligon, and Bird, "For most churches, multisite is a means to an end: helping people grow closer to God. Most multi-site churches don't make one campus the main deal and give the other venues or campuses second-class or overflow status."[6]

Structure

- It is estimated that there were about two hundred multisite churches in the U.S. in the 1990s, and by 2002 the number had grown to six hundred. In 2006, the number more than doubled to fifteen hundred, and by 2009, three thousand such churches existed in the United States.[7]

- Multisite churches are located in forty-seven U.S. states (and in the District of Columbia) and six Canadian provinces.

- Sizes of multisite churches range from attendance figures in the low hundreds to more than twenty thousand, with the median attendance of thirteen hundred.

- Two-thirds of multisite churches are a part of a denomination.

- Almost 50 percent of the churches use in-person teaching.

- About one-third of multisite churches have formed as a result of a merger with another church.

- 85 percent of multisite churches have three or fewer campuses and up to seven services.

- 88 percent of the campuses are within a thirty-minute drive from the original campus.

- 46 percent of multisite churches use almost all in-person teaching/preaching methods, 34 percent use a combination of in-person and video methods, and 20 percent use almost all video methods.

- The average beginning size of a new campus is 174 people.

- 50 percent of off-campus pastors were initially staff members of the original campus; 24 percent were lay leaders with the original campus.

- 23 percent of multisite churches offer a worship service in a language other than the one spoken at the original campus.[8]

- Average cost of launching a multisite campus in a low-risk, low-cost facility, such as a school or theater, is $250,000.[9]

- In 2009, about five million people (approximately 10 percent of Protestant worshippers) attended a multisite church in the United States or Canada.

- 37 percent of megachurches are multisite churches, up from 27 percent in 2005.[10]

- 66 percent of multisite churches report that the rate of conversion growth is happening either at the same rate or at a faster rate than at the original campus.[11]

History

While tracing the history of this movement, Brian Frye concluded: "It is difficult to pinpoint one specific event, time, place, or person as the key initiator of the multi-site church concept. The multi-site idea, though simple in many respects, developed via a more complex evolutionary process. The multi-site church model emerged progressively through the convergence of ideas, beliefs, social constructs, and technological advancements."[12]

Frye designated Elmer Towns as the "prime disseminator" of the multisite church with his writing on the extended geographic parish church, and Lyle Schaller, following Towns's work, is considered a "secondary herald of the multi-site church movement."[13]

In his 1990 publication, *10 of Today's Most Innovative Churches*, Towns shares the story of church planter Randy Pope, who started his ministry in Atlanta, Georgia, in 1977. In the chapter "An Extended Geographic Parish Church," Towns wrote: "Pope's original vision was to plant an innovative church that would have 100 different locations on the perimeter highway around Atlanta—it gets its name, Perimeter Church, from this vision. His burden was to reach the entire metropolitan area for Jesus Christ and influence its society. He knew he couldn't reach into every area of Atlanta so he prayed, 'Lord give us the perimeter.'"[14]

In another chapter, "One Church in Two Locations," Towns addressed the ministry of Mount Paran Church of God, also in Atlanta, Georgia. Towns noted that the church made the decision to minister in two physical locations when they outgrew their original campus. He wrote, "The church had grown so large on Mount Paran Road that there was absolutely no more room to build. Parking was saturated, they were busing people by shuttle from other parking lots and they had as many Sunday worship services (three) as humanly possible."[15] The church was able to purchase another campus 14.5 miles away, allowing them to reach more people.[16]

Another church profiled in this book was the Church On the Way in Van Nuys, California. This church also purchased another church's campus, making it their own so as to increase their ministry capacity.[17]

Towns described the multisite expression of local churches as a new phenomenon that was influenced by the technological improvements of transportation and communication devices that opened up opportunities for churches to grow in new ways. Rather than ministering to a limited parish, these churches were labeled as "extended geographical parish" churches across a much larger area, with the following characteristics:

- The church meets in several locations.
- The church operates different ministries in different locations.
- The church has expanded its location geographically in order to reach a larger local context.

Towns also explained this model as having "multiple ministries, multiple places of ministry, multiple ministers, but one central organization and one senior pastor."[18]

In his 1999 publication, *Discontinuity and Hope: Radical Change and the Path to the Future*, Lyle E. Schaller used the term "multisite" and "from one site to many."[19] He likened it to the branch banking model in the United States, where there is a central bank in the downtown area of the city and several branches scattered across the suburbs.

On September 11, 2001, the Leadership Network hosted a special forum on multisite churches in Chicago, Illinois, attended by sixty-five church leaders who were either already using the multisite model with their churches or were planning to implement the multisite model within the next year. Despite the news of the terrorist attacks, this meeting proved to be a significant event in the history of the Multisite Church Movement, for it offered an organized and focused gathering to discuss and learn from others engaged in this growing paradigm of ministry.[20] Since then, the Leadership Network has done much to raise awareness and equip others in the multisite model.

Numerous articles and books have been written addressing the topic of multisite churches in the twenty-first century. The multisite paradigm was so widespread that by 2009 Surratt, Ligon, and Bird were referring to the movement as "the new normal."[21] In a very short period of time, the word *multisite* had gone from obscurity to common parlance among many church leaders and churches in the United States.

Practices

There is no single approach to how multisite churches organize themselves and express themselves during their worship gatherings. Some churches only have worship gatherings at their newer campuses while others offer a wide range of ministry programs at the newer campuses. The worship expression at the campuses can be similar to that found at the original campus or can allow for a diversity of expressions. It is very common for the various sites to have live worship music and a campus pastor who is able to provide leadership and pastoral care to those who connect with the site. These campus pastors often relate to and serve under the oversight of a senior pastor. Offerings collected from each site are usually added to the church's general budget.

According to the Leadership Network, about 20 percent of multisite churches use only video methods when it comes to preaching. In other words, the message communicated during the gathering is recorded or brought in via a live feed from another campus (often the original campus); 34 percent of multisite churches use a combination of in-person preaching and video methods; 46 percent use almost all in-person preaching.[22]

Leaders

Influential multisite church leaders include J. Timothy Ahlen and J. V. Thomas, who were involved in developing the Key Church Strategy while ministering in Texas.[23] Other pioneers in the Multisite Church Movement include: Dino Rizzo (Healing Place Church), Wayne Cordeiro (New Hope Christian Fellowship), Greg Surratt (Seacoast Church), Dave Ferguson (Community Christian Church), Bobby Hill (New Life Christian Fellowship), Larry Osborne (North Coast Church), Jeffrey Johnson Sr. (Eastern Star Missionary Baptist), Kent Millard (St. Luke's United Methodist Church), Jim Wessel (Upper Arlington Lutheran Church), Randy Pope (Perimeter Church), Craig Groeschel (LifeChurch.TV), John Piper (Bethlehem Baptist Church), Dave Browning (Christ the King Community Church International), and Paul Walker (Mt. Paran Church of God).

Worldwide

Though this book focuses on the movement within the United States, it is worth mentioning that massive multisite churches have been in existence in other parts of the world as well. In his research published in 2000, Joel Comiskey made reference to the three largest "satellite cell churches" in the world. The largest church is the Works and Mission Baptist Church (Ivory Coast, Africa) with 150,000 in worship services and hundreds of satellites throughout the world, followed by Igreja Mana (Lisbon, Portugal). This church had 60,000 in worship services and 400 satellites. The third-largest church is New Life Fellowship (Bombay, India) with 50,000 in worship services and 250 satellites.[24]

Notes

1. Geoff Surratt, Greg Ligon, and Warren Bird, *The Multi-Site Church Revolution: Being One Church In Many Locations* (Grand Rapids: Zondervan, 2006), 11.
2. http://articles.chicagotribune.com/2005-01-16/features/0501160496_1_churches-evangelicals-bed-bath; accessed 10/25/2011; and http://www.npr.org/templates/story/story.php?storyId=4788676.
3. Bill Easum and Dave Travis, *Beyond the Box: Innovative Churches That Work* (Loveland, CO: Group, 2003), 85.
4. Scott McConnell, *Multi-Site Churches: Guidance for the Movement's Next Generation* (Nashville: B&H, 2009), 17.
5. Surratt, Ligon, and Bird, *The Multi-Site Church Revolution*, 18.
6. Geogg Surratt, Greg Ligon, and Warren Bird, *A Multi-Site Church Road Trip* (Grand Rapids: Zondervan, 2009), 12.
7. Ibid., 217.
8. Warren Bird and Kristin Walters, "Multisite Is Multiplying," Leadership Network (2010), http://leadnet.org/resources/download/multisite_is_multiplying_new_developments_in_the_movements_expansion/; accessed October 25, 2011.
9. Jim Tomberlin, "125 Tips for Multisite Churches and Those Who Want to Be," 10, March 8, 2011. Available from http://multisitesolutions

.com/blog/125-tips-for-multisite-churches; accessed October 26, 2011.

10. Brian Nathaniel Frye, "The Multi-Site Church Phenomenon in North America: 1950–2010," PhD diss., The Southern Baptist Theological Seminary, 2011, 303.

11. Elmer Towns, *10 of Today's Most Innovative Churches: What They're Doing, How They're Doing It, and How You Can Apply Their Ideas in Your Church* (Ventura, CA: Regal, 1990), 90.

12. Surratt, Ligon, and Bird, *A Multi-Site Church Road Trip*, 14.

13. Stephen Shields, "2007 Survey of 1,000 Multi-Site Churches," Leadership Network (January 31, 2007), 4; http://leadnet.org /resources/download/2007_survey_of_1000_multi-site_churches/; accessed December 29, 2011.

14. Frye, "The Multi-Site Church Phenomenon in North America," 32.

15. Towns, *10 of Today's Most Innovative Churches*, 166.

16. Ibid., 167.

17. Ibid., 72.

18. Ibid., 238.

19. Lyle E. Schaller, *Discontinuity and Hope: Radical Change and the Path to the Future* (Nashville: Abingdon, 1999), 174–79.

20. Dave Travis, "Multiple-Site/Multiple-Campus Churches," Leadership Network, August 11, 2003, http://leadnet.org/resources/download /multi-site_special_report; accessed December 29, 2011.

21. Surratt, Ligon, and Bird, *A Multi-Site Church Road Trip*.

22. Warren Bird and Kristin Walters, "Multisite Is Multiplying," Leadership Network (September 2, 2010), 17; http://leadnet.org/resources /download/multisite_is_multiplying_new_developments_in_the_ movements_expansion/; accessed December 29, 2011.

23. See J. Timothy Ahlen and J. V. Thomas, *One Church, Many Congregations: The Key Church Strategy* (Nashville: Abingdon, 1999).

24. Joel Comiskey, "Ten Largest Cell Churches," http://joelcomiskeygroup .com/articles/worldwide/tenLargest.htm; accessed December 29, 2011.

Additional Resources

In addition to these books, Leadership Network has several articles available to download on the topic of multisite churches that may be found at http://www.leadnet.org.

Easum, Bill, and Dave Travis. *Beyond the Box: Innovative Churches That Work.*

Loveland, CO: Group, 2003.

McConnell, Scott. *Multi-Site Churches: Guidance for the Movement's Next Generation*. Nashville: B&H, 2009.

Surratt, Geoff, Greg Ligon, and Warren Bird. *The Multi-Site Church Revolution: Being One Church ... In Many Locations*. Grand Rapids, MI: Zondervan, 2006.

———. *A Multi-Site Church Road Trip*. Grand Rapids: Zondervan, 2009.

11

Purpose Driven Church Movement

One of the most influential developments among evangelicals in the last thirty years has been the Purpose Driven Church Movement. What began with the birth of a church in Southern California in 1980 has expanded to include a network of churches in 162 countries.[1] Over two hundred thousand leaders across the globe have been trained in the purpose driven philosophy[2].

Definition

According to Rick Warren, the originator of the Purpose Driven Church Movement, "every church is driven by something." While such drives often come in the form of traditions, personalities, finances, programs, buildings, events, or seekers, Warren advocates that churches should be driven by the biblical purposes of evangelism, worship, discipleship, fellowship, and ministry.[3] According to him churches must develop systems and structures to balance themselves properly around these five areas.[4] From these convictions, Warren developed a strategy to reach people and move them from unbelievers to becoming regular church attendees and members of the church, to grow in their faith, to become ministers, and then return them to the field to reach other unbelievers with the gospel.[5]

Warren described the value and importance of being a Purpose Driven church:

- If you want to have a healthy physical body, you don't have to guess about how to get in shape—you can follow guidelines or models that include a well-balanced diet and exercise. To grow a healthy church, you don't have to guess either. The purpose driven paradigm is a church health model to help your church get in shape to live out its God-given purposes.

- The purpose driven model offers leaders in your church a unique, biblically based approach to help them establish, transform, or maintain a balanced, growing congregation. What is a balanced, growing congregation? It's one that is growing larger in numbers as it grows deeper in carrying out the God-given purposes for churches through worship, fellowship, discipleship, ministry, and missions.[6]

The purpose driven model not only assists church leaders in understanding the biblical purposes for the church but teaches them how to communicate those purposes to the church and organize the church around those purposes. Much of the model is designed around the need to understand the lifestyles and worldviews of the unbelievers the church is trying to reach, how to gather a crowd of people to attend a seeker-sensitive service, and strengthening the overall church.

History

The beginning of the movement can be traced back to when church planters Rick and Kay Warren arrived in the Saddleback

Valley of Southern California in 1979. On Easter Sunday 1980, Saddleback Valley Community Church had its first public worship service. What began with Warren's family has grown to become a church of twenty-two thousand people.[7]

Warren began training others in his approach to church planting and growth and by 1995 had compiled the story of the church and his purpose driven model in the book *The Purpose Driven Church: Growth Without Compromising Your Message and Mission*. This work has been has been listed as one of the one hundred Christian books that changed the twentieth century. Rich Karlgaard, writing for *Forbes*, described it as "the best book on entrepreneurship, business, and investment that I've read in some time."[8]

Warren was named one of the world's one hundred most influential people by *Time* magazine. In 2004 his book, *The Purpose Driven Life*, was published, selling more than twenty-two million copies and translated into twenty-eight languages.[9] The book has been called the best-selling hardback book of all time, according to *U.S. News & World Report*.[10]

Originator

Rick Warren, as originator, main leader, and representative of the movement, has had enormous influence on evangelicals, particularly in the areas of church planting and church health. It was the influence of the Church Growth Movement (see chapter 2), specifically that of the missiology of Donald McGavran, that served as a major force in guiding Warren's early steps toward Southern California and influencing the ideas that would develop into the Purpose Driven Church Movement. According to Warren, "God used the writings of Donald McGavran to sharpen my focus from pastoring an already established church to planting the church that I would pastor." After first being introduced to McGavran through an article he read while serving as a student missionary in Japan,

Warren wrote "I felt God directing me to invest the rest of my life discovering the principles—biblical, cultural, and leadership principles—that produce healthy, growing churches."[11]

For years, Warren and others have been engaged in training church planters and pastors in the purpose driven model. Numerous church planters and denominations use many elements of this model in their ministries. Pastors began to study the contents of *The Purpose Driven Church* and began to make application to their established churches. Lyle E. Schaller described the book as "the best book I've ever read on how to do church in today's world."[12]

Beliefs

The emphasis of the Purpose Driven Church Movement is on leaders and churches discovering the biblical purposes of the church. While new churches can begin with a clear purpose, Warren advocated that "absolutely nothing will revitalize a discouraged church faster than rediscovering its purpose."[13] A clear purpose builds morale, reduces frustration, allows concentration, attracts cooperation, and assists in evaluation.[14] Church planters and churches are encouraged to examine the Scriptures in an attempt to answer the following questions:

- Why does the church exist?

- What are we to be as a church? (Who and what are we?)

- What are we to do as a church? (What does God want done in the world?)

- How are we to do it?[15]

This model is centered upon two passages from the Bible: the Great Commandment (Matt. 22:37–40) and the Great Commission (Matt. 28:19–20). Warren wrote, "These two passages summarize everything we do at Saddleback Church. If an activity or program fulfills one of these commands, we do it. If it doesn't, we don't. We are driven by the Great Commandment and the Great Commission."[16] It is from these passages that the five purposes of the purpose driven church are developed.

The first purpose is worship, or to love the Lord with all your heart. The second is ministry, to love one's neighbor as oneself. The third purpose is related to evangelism. The Great Commission commands that the church go and make disciples. The fourth purpose is fellowship. Warren said that he believes that the command to baptize is symbolic of fellowship, or the identification with the body of Christ. The final purpose is discipleship. The church is commanded to teach believers to obey all that Christ commanded. According to Warren, "Today our purposes are unchanged: The church exists to edify, encourage, exalt, equip, and evangelize. While each church will differ in how these tasks are accomplished, there should be no disagreement about what we are called to do.[17]

Warren's inspirational story of the birth, growth, and global influence of Saddleback Community Church propelled the Purpose Driven Church Movement forward. His ability to summarize and effectively communicate vision, mission, and strategic processes to others has resulted in thousands of church leaders from across the globe embracing the purpose driven paradigm and implementing its philosophy into their ministries. *U.S. News & World Report* quoted management theorist Peter Drucker, who described Saddleback's organizational model as "'the most significant sociological [phenomenon] of the second half of the [twentieth] century.'"[18]

Notes

1. http://www.rickwarren.com/about/rickwarren/; accessed December 9, 2011.

2. http://www.rickwarren.com/about/saddlebackchurch/; accessed December 9, 2011.
3. Rick Warren, *The Purpose Driven Church* (Grand Rapids: Zondervan, 1995), 77, 78, 79, 80, 119.
4. Ibid., 122, 128.
5. Ibid., 130.
6. http://www.rickwarren.com/about/purposedriven/; accessed December 9, 2011.
7. http://www.rickwarren.com/about/rickwarren/; accessed December, 2011.
8. Rich Karlgaard, "Purpose Driven," Forbes.com, February 16, 2004, http://www.forbes.com/forbes/2004/0216/039.html.
9. Sonja Steptoe, "Rick Warren: A Pastor with a Purpose," *Time*, April 18, 2005, 108.
10. Jeffery L. Sheler, "Preacher with a Purpose," *U.S. News & World Report*, October 31, 2005, 54.
11. Rick Warren, *The Purpose Driven Church* (Grand Rapids: Zondervan, 1995), 29, 30.
12. Lyle Schaller, endorsement to *The Purpose Driven Church*.
13. Warren, *The Purpose Driven Church*, 82.
14. Ibid., 86, 87, 88, 91, 93.
15. Ibid., 98.
16. Ibid., 103.
17. Ibid., 103, 104, 105–7.
18. Sheler, "Preacher with a Purpose," 52.

Additional Resources

Searcy, Nelson, and Kerrick Thomas. *Launch: Starting a New Church from Scratch*. Ventura, CA: Regal, 2006.

Warren, Rick. *The Purpose Driven Church: Growth Without Compromising Your Message and Mission*. Grand Rapids: Zondervan, 1995.

_____. *The Purpose Driven Life*. Grand Rapids: Zondervan, 1995.

12

Seeker Movement

In the 1970s and 1980s, many U.S. church leaders began to speak in terms of the need for churches to act like missionaries within their own communities. While few used the word "contextualization," pastors began to consider seriously the importance of how to understand, connect with, and communicate effectively to unbelieving Americans. It was out of this environment that the Seeker Movement emerged. New forms of church service and other activities were offered with the seeker in mind.

The influence of the movement had profound effects on churches across the United States. Commenting on the movement, Dan Kimball wrote:

> Even if a church did not fully embrace a seeker-sensitive strategy, many churches at least adopted many of its contemporary approaches to ministry. The emphasis on creating a place for seekers to come meant emphasizing the weekend service as the entry point to the church. Contemporary architecture was developed for worship buildings along with new approaches to preaching and communication. Dramas, videos, and production staff were added to larger churches to help make the weekend services more professional. Even Garth Brooks-like headset microphones were used to show that we really are keeping up with the times and are hip to current culture.[1]

Definitions

Seeker Sensitive. Churches recognized that there would often be unbelievers present during weekly worship gatherings. Churches became "seeker sensitive" to accommodate these nonbelievers. Seeker-sensitive churches recognized that such people often had to overcome significant cultural and social barriers in order to be present; they often showed up with fears, hurts, and concerns related to gathering in a strange building with strangers to have a spiritual experience. Seeker-sensitive churches were proactive in alleviating these problems. These churches often spoke in language that outsiders would understand, or at least provided definitions when they used insider language. Theological concepts were explained rather than simply stated. Churches attempted to remove any surprises; at the beginning of the services, someone would explain to everyone present what would take place during the gathering. Nonmembers who were present would be referred to as "guests" rather than "visitors," and they were not asked to remain seated while the members "stand in your honor." Nothing was done to make the outsiders feel out of place or that would make them feel they were in an unwelcoming environment.

Seeker Driven. A term that was closely related to *seeker sensitive*, and sometimes equated with it and the movement as a whole, was "seeker driven." Churches that were seeker driven designed their entire weekly gatherings as an event for the unbeliever and outsider. This usually meant that the church had to have a separate weekly gathering for believers, as the seeker service was more akin to an evangelistic rally. While the philosophy of being seeker sensitive was behind seeker-driven services, unlike a seeker-sensitive worship gathering—which was designed primarily for the church members to worship God—a seeker-driven event would be entertaining and with little expectation for the participants, with the entire focus on the unbeliever. Secular music was common, as was the use of drama and messages that were evangelistic and apologetic in nature.

History

One of the most influential churches in the movement was Willow Creek Community Church (South Barrington, Illinois). In 1975, Bill Hybels and friends began a worship service in the Willow Creek Theater in Palatine, Illinois.[2] Over the next thirty-five years they would pioneer numerous approaches to engage unbelievers in seeker-sensitive and seeker-driven fashions, making the church synonymous with the Seeker Movement. In 1996, G. A. Pritchard began his book about the church by noting its influence: "Willow Creek is leading a worldwide movement. Attending a recent Willow Creek training conference in South Barrington, Illinois, were over 2,300 church leaders from Australia, the Bahamas, Canada, England, Holland, Honduras, India, Japan, Korea, Mexico, Norway, Scotland, Sweden, the United States, and Venezuela. Since 1988, Willow Creek has sponsored Christian Leadership conferences in the United States, England, Wales, France, Australia, and New Zealand with an attendance of more than 50,000 individuals. Willow Creek is currently shaping how church is 'done' for thousands of churches."[3]

The birth and first decades of the church began with the bad experiences that Bill and Lynne Hybels had whenever they brought an unbelieving friend to their church's worship gathering. "If you had grown up in the church and were accustomed to the routine, you were fine. But it was no place for the unchurched,"[4] Bill said. In the mid-1970s, Hybels, leading a weekly youth event specifically designed for evangelism, promised the young people that if they would bring their unbelieving friends to a major outreach service, he would provide clear gospel presentation. Nearly six hundred students attended with many taking the opportunity to place their faith in Christ. For Hybels this event was a critical moment in time, when he came to the realization that a weekly service designed for unbelievers was necessary and fruitful. He became committed to the idea of seeker services aimed at the unbeliever.

When Willow Creek Community Church was later started, the Hybelses formed a weekly seeker service "that would provide a safe and informative place where unchurched people could come to investigate Christianity."[5]

They developed a vision statement for a church to become "a biblically functioning community" with the mission "to turn irreligious people into fully devoted followers of Christ." Their strategy for accomplishing this mission and vision included:

1. Building an authentic relationship with a nonbeliever.
2. Sharing a verbal witness.
3. Bringing the seeker to a service designed especially for them.
4. Regularly attending a service for believers.
5. Joining a small group.
6. Discovering, developing, and deploying your spiritual gift.
7. Stewarding your resources in a God-honoring way.[6]

In summary, Hybels approached the development and execution of a service much like a Billy Graham evangelistic crusade, just on a smaller scale. A church for the unchurched was developed with weekend services that were marketed widely to attract the unbeliever. These services were to be entertaining, thought-provoking, requiring limited participation, providing a crowd for the seeker's anonymity, and a gospel presentation with the goal of attracting seekers to the movement.

Practices

Churches involved in this movement differ in the degree to which they relate to the seeker in their gatherings, and a spectrum of belief and practices could be found throughout the movement:

Seeker Driven	Seeker Sensitive

While Willow Creek Community Church is closer to the seeker-driven side of the spectrum, a church such as Saddleback Church in Southern California would lean in the direction of being seeker sensitive (see chapter 11). In fact, Rick Warren warns churches that while seeker sensitivity is healthy, he does not think it appropriate for churches to become seeker driven. "Attracting seekers is the first step in the process of making disciples, but it should not be the driving force of the church. While it is fine for a business to be market driven (give the customer whatever he wants), a church has a higher calling. The church should be seeker sensitive but it must not be seeker driven."[7]

Though the characteristics of churches that are part of the Seeker Movement differ, the following generalizations are often found among them and are important to the movement:

Research. Churches are responsible for understanding the nonbelievers who live in their communities. In order to meet the needs of the people living in their communities, churches must first determine those needs. Formal and informal surveys and other research projects can be helpful in this process. It is after proper knowledge is gained that strategies can be developed to reach the community.

Marketing. Following the research collection process, churches should begin to advertise what they have to offer the community. This typically involves targeting a specific demographic or population segment of the community.

A significant development related to the movement was Willow Creek's profile of the stereotypical couple living in their community. In *Inside the Mind of Unchurched Harry and Mary*, Lee Strobel argues the need for churches to have a general understanding of the people they are trying to reach.[8] Rick Warren of the Saddleback Church also strongly advocated this approach in *The Purpose Driven Church*, where he recognized the need to know about "Saddleback Sam." For Warren, such understanding was not only related to doing a better job at evangelism, but also related to being seeker sensitive and not seeker driven.[9]

To develop an effective marketing strategy for evangelism, the church needed to have an understanding of the lifestyle and world-view of the unbelievers. Using his experiences and research findings, Strobel shares the following general characteristics of the stereotypical "unchurched Harry and Mary" among the people in his community:

1. Harry has rejected church, but that doesn't necessarily mean he has rejected God.
2. Harry is morally adrift, but he secretly wants an anchor.
3. Harry resists rules but responds to reasons.
4. Harry doesn't understand Christianity, but he's also ignorant about what he claims to believe in.
5. Harry has legitimate questions about spiritual matters, but he doesn't expect answer from Christians.
6. Harry doesn't just ask, "Is Christianity true?" Often, he's asking: "Does Christianity work?"
7. Harry doesn't just want to know something; he wants to experience it.
8. Harry doesn't want to be somebody's project, but he would like to be somebody's friend.

9. Harry may distrust authority, but he's receptive to authentic biblical leadership.
10. Harry is no longer loyal to denominations, but he is attracted to places where his needs will be met.
11. Harry isn't much of a joiner, but he's hungry for a cause he can connect with.
12. Even if Harry's not spiritually sensitive, he wants his children to get quality moral training.
13. Harry and Mary are confused about sex roles, but they don't know that the Bible can clarify for them what it means to be a man and woman.
14. Harry is proud that he's tolerant of different faiths, but he thinks Christians are narrow-minded.
15. There's a good chance Harry would try church if a friend invited him—but this may actually do more harm than good.[10]

Personal and Corporate Evangelism. Being seeker sensitive extended beyond corporate gatherings to the lifestyles of believers. Church members were to share the gospel with unbelievers in their circles of influence and then invite them to a church gathering where they would hear a professionally communicated gospel.

Seeker Service. A seeker service was a major characteristic of the Seeker Movement. Churches were to use their research findings to support and develop a service primarily designed for seekers where they could hear the gospel presented in an environment that was entertaining, engaging, and prepared with the unbeliever in mind.

One of the earlier books from the perspective of the movement was Ed Dobson's *Starting a Seeker-Sensitive Service*. In this work, Dobson shares his experience in leading his church to becoming seeker-sensitive during the mid-1980s.

As the senior pastor of Calvary Church I became concerned that our ministry was not reaching unchurched people. We were reaching many people from religious backgrounds, but not many hard-core skeptics. I asked several friends to join me in exploring how we could start a ministry that would be geared to the needs of people who have lived outside religious circles. We spent nearly a year reading, researching, and deciding what we should do.

What happened? Five years ago we began a service on Saturday night that we called "Saturday Night—A Place to Answer Questions." The format is non- (almost anti-) traditional. The music is contemporary rock and roll. We use drama. The dress code is blue jeans and T-shirts. The format is informal. I give a talk (sermon) while sitting on a bar stool (renamed a church stool), and at the end of the talk I receive written questions from the audience. That is—and is not—about all there is to it.[11]

Future

Though few evangelical conversations regarding the Seeker Movement are occurring today, some recent attention has been directed toward the effects of the movement over the years.

Kent Carlson and Mike Lueken, formerly outspoken leaders within the Seeker Movement, have written about their concerns

Concerns About the Seeker Movement

A pervasive focus in the religious culture throughout North America is that success lies in attracting people, churched and unchurched, to their particular church organization. This attractional model, we believe, is fundamentally flawed and will not be able to produce in any significant way the kind of Christ followers church leaders want to produce. . . . We also began to grow increasingly uneasy that this model of doing church might be unhealthy for the people whose understanding of the Christian life was shaped by a church culture that treated them as religious consumers.[12]

with the movement. Even Hybels himself made a public declaration that the approach used by Willow Creek was not working to see people grow to deep levels of maturity in their faith. While the Seeker Movement was effective at bringing large numbers of people to Jesus, the movement lacked the ability to maintain them.[13]

Notes

1. Dan Kimball, *The Emerging Church: Vintage Christianity for New Generations* (Grand Rapids: Zondervan, 2003), 103.
2. http://willowcreek.org/aboutwillow/willow-history; accessed November 28, 2011.
3. G. A. Pritchard, *Willow Creek Seeker Services: Evaluating a New Way of Doing Church* (Grand Rapids: Baker, 1996), 11.
4. Lynne and Bill Hybels, *Rediscovering Church: The Story and Vision of Willow Creek Community Church* (Grand Rapids: Zondervan, 1995), 31.
5. Ibid., 39, 40, 41.
6. Ibid., 169, 170, 172, 175, 177, 178, 179.
7. Rick Warren, *The Purpose Driven Church: Growth Without Compromising Your Message and Mission* (Grand Rapids: Zondervan 1995), 79–80.
8. Lee Strobel, *Inside the Mind of Unchurched Harry and Mary: How to Reach Friends and Family Who Avoid God and the Church* (Grand Rapids: Zondervan, 1993).
9. Warren, *The Purpose Driven Church*, 169.
10. Strobel, *Inside the Mind of Unchurched Harry and Mary*. For this list and a thorough discussion of each point, see chapters 4 and 5.
11. Ed Dobson, *Starting a Seeker Sensitive Service: How Traditional Churches Can Reach the Unchurched* (Grand Rapids: Zondervan, 1993), 7.
12. Kent Carlson and Mike Lueken, *Renovation of the Church: What Happens When a Seeker Church Discovers Spiritual Formation* (Downers Grove, IL: InterVarsity, 2011), 26, 28.
13. Bill Hybels, foreword, in *Move: What 1000 Churches Reveal About Spiritual Growth* by Greg L. Hawkins and Cally Parkinson (Grand Rapids: Zondervan, 2011), 9–10.

Additional Resources

Carlson, Kent and Mike Lueken. *Renovation of the Church: What Happens When a Seeker Church Discovers Spiritual Formation.* Downers Grove, IL: IVP, 2011.

Dobson, Ed. *Starting a Seeker Sensitive Service: How Traditional Churches Can Reach the Unchurched.* Grand Rapids: Zondervan, 1993.

Hawkins, Greg L., and Cally Parkinson. *Move: What 1000 Churches Reveal About Spiritual Growth.* Grand Rapids: Zondervan, 2011.

Hybels, Lynne, and Bill Hybels. *Rediscovering Church: The Story and Vision of Willow Creek Community Church.* Grand Rapids: Zondervan, 1995.

Hybels, Bill, and Mark Mittelberg. *Becoming a Contagious Christian.* Grand Rapids: Zondervan, 1994.

Pritchard, G. A. *Willow Creek Seeker Services: Evaluating a New Way of Doing Church.* Grand Rapids: Baker, 1996.

Strobel, Lee. *Inside the Mind of Unchurched Harry and Mary: How to Reach Friends and Family Who Avoid God and the Church.* Grand Rapids: Zondervan, 1993.

Warren, Rick, *The Purpose Driven Church: Growth Without Compromising Your Message and Mission.* Grand Rapids: Zondervan, 1995.

13

Short-Term Missions Movement

Over the past couple of decades, the number of individuals and churches involved in short-term missionary activities outside of the United States has increased greatly. These trips range from two weeks (or even a single day) to two years or longer. Travels that were once considered exotic and unlikely are now happening on an annual basis. Some argue that such trips are little more than glorified vacations that interfere with the daily work of long-term missionaries, while others make the case that short-term missions are strongly beneficial to every party involved. Regardless, one thing is certain: Americans have become significantly involved in such labors, and the increased numbers of those engaged in them and the amount of money spent annually is evidence of this fact.

Robert Wuthnow estimated that in 2001 there were 350,000 Americans who had spent from two weeks to one year serving as short-term mission volunteers and that up to one million people had served less than two weeks outside of the country.[1] Wuthnow also notes that the churches of the Southern Baptist Convention report that more than 150,000 of their members go on annual short-term trips. The United Methodist Church records sending 100,000 members. In support of the rising interest in short-term missions, Wuthnow indicates that "12 percent of active churchgoers who were in high school youth groups since 2000 have gone overseas on a mission trip, and that figure is up from only 5 percent among churchgoers who were teens in the 1990s, 4 percent of those who were teens in the 1980s, and only 2 percent before that."[2] Wuthnow estimates that Americans spend $1.6 billion on short-term mission trips each year.[3]

Others have attempted to quantify the numbers of those involved today. According to Robert J. Priest, Terry Dischinger, Steve Rasmussen, and C. M. Brown, "there is good reason to believe that more than one and a half million U. S. Christians travel abroad each year on 'short-term mission trips,' with an additional unknown number traveling on similar mission trips within the United States."[4]

History

One of the histories on the movement was written by anthropologist Brian Howell in "Roots of the Short-Term Missionary 1960–1985."[5] Following World War II, a large number of young Christians showed a zeal for missions, and Youth with a Mission (YWAM) and Operation Mobilization (OM) started developing new ways to mobilize and deploy them. These innovative programs allowed the young adults to operate in the field for shorter periods of time, yet still get the mission experience.

During the 1960s other mission organizations began to develop their own short-term models. By the 1970s, churches were organizing short-term trips for their congregations apart from mission agencies, denominations, and other parachurch organizations. The numbers involved began to swell. By the 1990s, youth pastors were expected to plan and take youth groups on such trips each year. It has been recently suggested that the Short-Term Missions Movement may be going through a period of transition, one from international involvement to domestic trips. Ken Walker noted that overseas trips have decreased by 15 percent since 2008, while Missions Data International shows that inquiries for domestic trips have increased steadily over the past four years.[6]

Missiologists A. Scott Moreau, Gary R. Corwin, and Gary B. McGee claim that today "short-term mission trips are as common as high school proms."[7] What started as a phenomenon to employ young people following World War II has grown to encompass people of all ages and diverse backgrounds. Moreau, Corwin, and McGee offer the following commonalities among most short-term trips being taken today:

- The majority of the trips are being conducted by churches and not mission agencies.

- The typical length of each trip spans one to two weeks.

- The median age of the participants is under twenty.

- The primary purpose of the mission is focused on the spiritual growth and development of the participants rather than the team's contribution to the Lord's work in the other country.

- Many missiological principles are being violated and large sums of money are being spent without many positive results.[8]

By the turn of the century, the movement had grown to such proportions that it was necessary to develop a set of ethical guidelines and an accreditation process for those involved in sending, receiving, facilitating, and supporting short-term missions. Concern with the observation of Moreau, Corwin, and McGee that violations to missiological principles were occurring, in addition to the desire for encouragement, excellence, and accountability, led a group of short-term mission leaders from the United States to begin working on establishing a set of ethical guidelines. Similar codes of conduct had already been developed in the United Kingdom and Canada. Over a two-year period this group consulted with five mission networks and more than four hundred mission leaders to develop the "U. S. Standards of Excellence in Short-Term Mission" in 2003.[9] Seven standards were set down to promote excellence in the field of short-term missions:

- **God-Centeredness**. An excellent short-term mission gives primacy to God's glory and his kingdom.

- **Empowering Partnerships**. An excellent short-term mission establishes healthy, interdependent, ongoing relationships between sending and receiving partners.

- **Mutual Design**. An excellent short-term mission collaboratively plans each specific program for the benefit of all participants.

- **Comprehensive Administration**. An excellent short-term mission exhibits integrity through reliable set-up and administration for all participants.

- **Qualified Leadership**. An excellent short-term mission screens, trains, and develops capable leadership.

- **Appropriate Training**. An excellent short-term mission prepares and equips all participants for the mission.

- **Thorough Follow-Up**. An excellent short-term mission requires debriefing and appropriate follow-up for all participants.[10]

Controversy

While evangelicals are generally in agreement that there is value in the Short-Term Missions Movement, debates regarding the benefits of the movement to the advancement of the gospel continue. Questions have been raised regarding the stewardship of such large amounts of money for short-term activities and whether it would be better to send such money to the communities themselves. Some advocate that while the use of short-term trips does little to benefit the communities, such trips are of great benefit to the participants in their kingdom service and growth in Christ. Discussions have occurred as to whether or not such activities are truly "mission" work, and whether or not a short-term laborer can be legitimately labeled as a "missionary." Arguments have been made that while there is kingdom value in short-term trips, this has led to the "amateurization" of the missionary vocation. Others have attempted to show how short-term missions can complement long-term missions. Whatever the arguments, two things appear to be certain about the movement: short-term trips will continue to take place and debates will continue regarding the strengths and limitations of such trips.

Future

Many of the conclusions drawn regarding the strengths and limitations of short-term missions are based on anecdotal evidence and assumptions. Prior to 2003, very little research had been conducted on short-term missions.[11] To date, two general types of research have been produced: the first category addresses the benefits of short-term missions to the individual and to the sending church. Such research typically examines issues such as the short-termer's possible growth in Christ, increased financial contributions to missions, and the likelihood of short-term trips resulting in long-term missionary service. The second type of research examines the effectiveness of the actual work itself on the field missionaries and indigenous churches. Even though the research is limited in both areas, the churches that tend to make a great contribution to the Lord's work through short-term missions manifest the following characteristics:

- They have a commitment to relate their mission to what is happening in the host country.

- They have a commitment to developing strong relationships by returning to work with the same people in the same areas year after year.

- They have a commitment to learn good missiology so as to avoid unnecessary errors.[12]

In his assessment of several of the research findings that have been published, C. M. Brown offered the following conclusions:

It is not entirely clear that STM (short-term missions) makes a strategic commitment to missions. STM may result in the creation of highly valued "bridging" social capital if participants will maintain lasting contact. The contact can be largely positive, but there is evidence that it often is not.

STM participants can be changed, but research-based evidence that the changes are lasting is in short supply. STM must include serious pre-field training and orientation on culture-related topics, coaching on the field, and debriefing and long-term follow-up; otherwise, hopes of long-term change in participants through STM appear to be in vain.

The STM phenomenon may be contributing to a decline in long-term missions. Missiologists should research. Little research addresses the impact of STM on host nationals.[13]

Recognizing that there is great potential in this movement, Brown, along with Robert J. Priest, Terry Dischinger, and Steve Rasmussen, noted in another article that "STM does not appear to be realizing this potential. We need to revise and clarify our goals, submit our claims to a process of research and testing, and devise the right sorts of research to help modify our ministry practices in God-honoring ways."[14]

Notes

1. Robert Wuthnow, *Boundless Faith: The Global Outreach of American Churches* (Berkeley, CA: University of California Press, 2009), 23.
2. Ibid., 167.
3. Ibid., 180.
4. Robert J. Priest, *et al.*, "Researching the Short-Term Mission Movement," *Missiology* 34, no. 4 (October 2006), 432.
5. Brian Howell, "Roots of the Short-Term Missionary 1960–1985," Building Church Leaders, March 5, 2006, http://www .buildingchurchleaders.com/articles/2006/rootsmissionary.html; accessed October 20, 2011.
6. Ken Walker, "Homeward Bound?" *Christianity Today* 54, no. 6 (June 2010), 15.
7. A. Scott Moreau, Gary R. Corwin, and Gary B. McGee, *Introducing World Missions: A Biblical, Historical, and Practical Survey* (Grand Rapids: Baker, 2004), 254.
8. Ibid.
9. The website for the accrediting and resourcing body is http://www.soe .org/explore/. On the history, see "Historical Development of the U.S. Standards of Excellence in Short-Term Mission," http://www.soe.org /explore/wp-content/uploads/2011/09/SOE_History_Detailed.pdf; accessed December 30, 2011.
10. "Overview: The Seven Standards of Excellence in Short-Term Mission," http://www.soe.org/explore/wp-content/uploads/2011/09 /7-Standards-Brief.pdf; accessed December 30, 2011.
11. Robert J. Priest, ed., *Effective Engagement in Short-Term Missions: Doing It Right!* (Pasadena, CA: William Carey Library, 2008), v.
12. Moreau, Corwin, and McGee, *Introducing World Missions*, 254.

13. C. M. Brown, "Field Statement on the Short-Term Mission Phenomenon: Contributing Factors and Current Debate," 25–26, June 9, 2005, http://web.tiu.edu/files/divinity/academics/programs/phd /ics/stm_field_statement.pdf; accessed December 30, 2011.

14. Priest *et al.*, "Researching the Short-Term Mission Movement," 445

Additional Resources

Dearborn, Tim. *Short-Term Missions Workbook: From Mission Tourists to Global Citizens*. Downers Grove, IL: IVP, 2003.

Forward, David C. *The Essential Guide to the Short-Term Mission Trip*. Chicago: Moody, 1998.

Livermore, David A. *Serving with Eyes Wide Open: Doing Short-Term Missions with Cultural Intelligence*. Grand Rapids: Baker, 2006.

Peterson, Roger, Gordon Aeschliman, and R. Wayne Sneed. *Maximum Impact Short-Term Mission: The God-Commanded, Repetitive Deployment of Swift, Temporary, Non-Professional Missionaries*. Minneapolis: STEMPress, 2003.

Priest, Robert J., ed. *Effective Engagement in Short-Term Missions: Doing It Right!* Pasadena, CA: William Carey Library, 2008.

Stiles, J. Mack, and Leann Stiles. *Mack and Leann's Guide to Short-Term Missions*. Downers Grove, IL: IVP, 2000.

Wilder, Michael S., and Shane W. Parker. *Transformission: Making Disciples Through Short-Term Missions*. Nashville: B&H, 2010.

14

Spiritual Warfare Movement

Spiritual warfare includes all that is related to hindering a believer's growth in Christ and the evangelization of unbelievers. Such opposition comes from Satan and his demons (Rev. 12:9), the ungodly world system (1 John 5:4), and the flesh (Rom. 7:18). By the 1980s evangelicals started becoming more and more open to the notion of spiritual warfare and to learning techniques for dealing with satanic opposition. Numerous spiritual warfare conferences were offered, and publishers provided a multitude of books on the topic. Frank Peretti's fictional works *This Present Darkness* and *Piercing the Darkness* sold millions of copies while also serving as a catalyst to point the hearts and minds of evangelicals toward spiritual warfare. From within the academy, C. Peter Wagner of Fuller Theological Seminary spoke often on the topic and penned several related books. Schools such as Wheaton College and Trinity Evangelical Divinity School offered courses on spiritual warfare-related matters. During this time, at least twenty-five organizations in North America emphasized spiritual warfare, trained practitioners, or published literature on the topic.[1]

The movement was never monolithic, but rather encompassed different personalities, theological positions, and perspectives. Such diversity created an atmosphere for lively and intensive discussions.

Some began to advocate the importance of identifying the demons controlling cities or individuals, gaining knowledge from them, and casting them out in the name of Jesus. Others developed programs such as counseling ministries involving exorcisms, intercessory ministries, and prayer walking.

Both praise and criticism toward spiritual warfare proponents come from evangelical ranks. While the bringing of attention to the reality of satanic and demonic activity and to the importance of prayer was generally appreciated, concern that many within the movement were embracing animistic thinking and practices arose. There was also concern that biblical theology was being mixed with elements of spiritualism and animism to create a syncretistic way of understanding and overpowering the forces of hell.

Definitions

As with any movement, a new nomenclature has developed. Following are five terms that became common parlance among those involved in the movement.

- **Spiritual Warfare**. According to Ed Murphy, spiritual warfare is "war with sin and sinful personalities. While all human beings are victims of spiritual warfare, its primary combatants are God and His angels and children, who are opposed by Satan and his demons. It is warfare between the kingdom of God and the kingdom of the Devil."[2]

- **Spiritual Mapping**. A method of discerning the territorial spirits that involves conducting an extensive spiritual and religious historical analysis of the area.[3]

- **Territorial Spirits**. Demons that exercise authority over peoples, governments, countries, and cities.[4]

- **Power Encounter**. An event in which the powers of evil are tested against the power of God, usually resulting in conversion.[5]

- **Strategic-Level Warfare**. A strategy for overcoming high-level territorial spirits that involves: (1) discerning the territorial spirits; (2) dealing with the corporate sin of the area; and (3) engaging in warfare prayer against the demons.[6]

Beliefs

The diversity of the movement makes it difficult to provide specific details of the many perspectives in a single chapter. However, there are general foundational matters common to most of those involved in the movement. Charles E. Lawless notes that among the great diversity in the movement, common ground is found "in a consistent call to recognize Satan's wiles in order to break his power through appropriate warfare strategies."[7] Lawless gives a list of the foundational beliefs upon which those within the movement build their warfare strategies.[8]

The Literal Reality of Satan and Demons. Satan and his demonic hordes are real beings. Just as the Bible affirms a real God, it also reveals a real Satan and real demons.

The Continuing Battle Between God's Kingdom and Satan's Forces. While Christ has triumphed over the evil one, Satan is still active in the world today. Until he is cast into the lake of fire, he and his demons will continue to work to oppose God and God's kingdom.

The Offensive and Defensive Nature of Spiritual Warfare. Believers are to exercise Jesus' authority over the powers of evil as they make disciples of all nations. Just as Jesus went into the desert to do battle with Satan, his followers are to be active in binding

Satan and loosen the will of God to be done through prayer. Believers are also to be on the defense, to resist the devil, and to flee from temptation.

History

The Intercession Working Group of the Lausanne Committee for World Evangelization met in London July 10–14, 1993 to discuss the growing interest in spiritual warfare among evangelicals. The group developed an official statement for the Lausanne Movement regarding spiritual warfare.[9] According to the work of this group, the following four global shifts were the reasons for the rise of interest in this topic.

Change in Initiatives. The initiative in evangelization is passing to churches in the developing world. As people from the same background evangelize their own people, dealing with the powers of darkness has become a natural way of thinking and working. This is especially true of the rapidly growing Pentecostal churches.

Increased Interest in Eastern Religions. The spiritual bankruptcy of the West has opened up great interest in Eastern religions and even of drug cultures and has brought about a resurgence of the occult.

Influx of Non-Christian Worldview. The massive migrations of peoples from the Majority World to the West has brought a torrent of non-Christian worldviews and practices. Increasing mobility has also exposed developing countries to new fringe groups, cults, and freemasonry. These movements bring about an interest in the occult.

Sensationalism of the Occult. The secular media has dramatized and encouraged interest in occult ideas and practices with films such as The Exorcist. In Christian publishing, books by Frank Peretti and the spate of "How to" books on power evangelism and spiritual warfare have reflected a similar trend.[10]

Edward Rommen provides a brief history of the development of the movement in the book *Spiritual Power and Missions: Raising the Issues*. According to Rommen there are at least four historical paths that have converged and helped to create the Spiritual Warfare Movement.[11]

First, the general history of the church reveals interest regarding matters such as warfare prayer, power encounters, exorcisms, and healings. The movement is not a new creation.

Second, the specific history of missions reveals numerous examples of spiritual opposition and engagement. Spiritual manifestations and attacks are normative on the mission frontier. These events in the field came to be known as "power encounters" and required a proper response to overcome them.

Third, the recent development of missionary strategies resulted in creativity and an attempt to be more effective in gospel advancement. Some of the leaders of the Church Growth Movement were a major influence in this area (see chapter 2). In addition to using the social sciences for the growth of churches, strategists began asking how spiritual weapons could also be used to grow churches. For example, some began asking questions such as: What is the relationship of prayer to the growth of churches? and Can demons be identified over geographical areas and then exorcised so that the gospel can advance among the people?

Finally, recent renewal movements have placed emphasis on the miraculous. The explosive growth of Pentecostalism and the Charismatic Movement converged to help form the Signs and Wonders Movement (with influence from the Church Growth Movement) with the effect of encouraging discussion about spiritual warfare.

By the year 2000 interest and controversy among evangelicals piqued. In response, the Theology Strategy Working Group and the Intercession Working Group of the Lausanne Committee for World Evangelization and the Association of Evangelicals in Africa met in Nairobi for the "Deliver Us from Evil" consultation. It addressed matters related to spiritual conflict and warfare. The desired outcome of the gathering was to "get a Biblical and comprehensive understanding" of the enemy, how he is working, and how to fight him. Numerous papers were produced for and from this consultation.[12]

Leaders

While the movement includes many leaders concentrating on different aspects, some of the more influential and widely recognized authorities on spiritual warfare included: Cindy Jacobs, Mark Bubeck, C. Peter Wagner, Neil Anderson, George Otis, Charles Kraft, Edward F. Murphy, Tim Logan, and Timothy Warner.

Notes

1. Charles E. Lawless, "The Relationship Between Evangelism and Spiritual Warfare in the North American Spiritual Warfare Movement, 1986–1997," PhD diss., The Southern Baptist Theological Seminary, 1997, 1–3.
2. Ed Murphy, *The Handbook for Spiritual Warfare*, rev. ed. (Nashville: Thomas Nelson, 1992), 539.
3. Clinton E. Arnold, "The Powers" in A. Scott Moreau, *Evangelical Dictionary of World Missions* (Grand Rapids: Baker, 2000), 778.
4. Arnold, "Territorial Spirits," in *Evangelical Dictionary of World Missions*, 940.
5. Charles H. Kraft, "Power Encounter," in *Evangelical Dictionary of World Missions*, 774, 775.
6. Arnold, "The Powers" in Moreau, *Evangelical Dictionary of World Missions*, 778.
7. Lawless, "The Relationship Between Evangelism and Spiritual Warfare in the North American Spiritual Warfare Movement, 1986–1997," 5.
8. Ibid., 7–13.
9. http://www.lausanne.org/en/documents/all/consultation-statements/206-statement-on-spiritual-warfare-1993.html; accessed January 7, 2012.

10. Ibid.

11. Edward Rommen, ed., *Spiritual Power and Missions: Raising the Issues* (Pasadena, CA: William Carey Library, 1995), 2–4.

12. See http://www.lausanne.org/en/gatherings/issue-based/nairobi -2000.html and for the papers presented see http://www.lausanne.org /en/gatherings/issue-based/15-gatherings/nairobi-2000/180-deliver -us-from-evil-consultation-related-documents.html; accessed January 8, 2012.

Additional Resources

Arnold, Clinton E. *3 Crucial Questions About Spiritual Warfare.* Grand Rapids: Baker, 1997.

Lawless, Charles E. "The Relationship Between Evangelism and Spiritual Warfare in the North American Spiritual Warfare Movement, 1986–1997." PhD diss. The Southern Baptist Theological Seminary, 1997.

Lowe, Chuck. *Territorial Spirits and World Evangelization?* Great Britain: Mentor/OMF, 1998.

Murphy, Ed. *The Handbook for Spiritual Warfare.* Rev and updated ed. Nashville: Thomas Nelson, 1992.

Rommen, Edward, ed. *Spiritual Power and Missions: Raising the Issues.* Pasadena, CA: William Carey Library, 1995.

Wagner, C. Peter. *Warfare Prayer.* Ventura, CA: Regal, 1992.

Wimber, John, and Kevin Springer. *Power Evangelism.* London: Hodder and Stoughton, 1992.